Contents

NOTES

Topic 3: Skill Acquisition

What you need to learn:		Yes	Nearly	No
3.1: Coach and performer	3.1.1: Coaching styles to improve the performance of learners: command, reciprocal, guided discovery and problem solving.			
	3.1.2: The development of tactics and strategies in a competition or performance to optimise outcome.			
	3.1.3: Dissection of a skill in order to identify technical elements: preparation, execution and recovery phases leading to the correct result or outcome. Exploration of how to analyse a skill in order to identify any technical strengths and weaknesses. How to compare to higher-level performer.			
3.2: The classification and transfer of skills	3.2.1: Knowledge and understanding of skill classifications. Classification continuums as gross/fine, internally paced/externally paced, discrete/serial/continuous. The open/closed continuum in relation to the sporting environment, decision making and practice structure.			
	3.2.2: The uses of transfer of skills. Transfer as positive/negative, proactive/retroactive, bilateral and zero. Transfer as the effect of one skill on another as a result of practice/experience.			
3.3: Learning theories	3.3.1: The associative theories (classical and operant conditioning). Reinforcement —			

1

	positive, negative, punishment, stimulus–response (S–R) bond — and its use in skill learning.			
	3.3.2: Thorndike's three laws in relation to learning as effect, exercise and readiness and their application to practical situations.			
	3.3.3: Fitts and Posner's three stages of learning (cognitive, associative and autonomous). The characteristics and coaching requirements at each stage. The type and role of different types of feedback at each stage.			
3.4: Practices	**3.4.1:** Knowledge and understanding of practice methods and structure as a coach and for a performer and their impact on performance.			
	3.4.2: Practice methods as part, progressive part, whole, whole–part–whole. Practice structure as in massed, distributed, fixed and variable.			
3.5: Guidance	**3.5.1:** The types, purpose and effectiveness of guidance methods: visual, verbal, manual and mechanical. Visual guidance in the form of demonstration and visual materials. Verbal guidance in the form of knowledge of direct, indirect and prompting. Manual and mechanical guidance in the form of physical support and aids, restrictions and forced responses.			

	3.5.2: Uses of technology to underpin guidance methods in order to optimise performance, e.g. to measure, monitor and evaluate performance.			
3.6: Feedback	**3.6.1**: The types, purposes and effectiveness of feedback as motivation, reinforcement and detection and correction of errors.			
	3.6.2: Types of feedback as in positive/negative, knowledge of performance, knowledge of results, concurrent/terminal, intrinsic/extrinsic.			
	3.6.3: Uses of technology to support types of feedback in order to optimise performance.			
	3.6.4: Open and closed loop control Open loop models to include input, executive system, effector system and output. Closed loop control models — input, executive system, effector system, output and feedback. Application of when each loop could be used.			
3.7: Memory models	**3.7.1**: Information processing Components of information processing, including: input, stimulus identification, perception and selective attention, response selection, response programming, output — based on the models of Welford and Whiting. Detection, comparison and recognition (DCR) phases.			
	3.7.2: The three memory systems as short-term sensory store (STSS), short-term memory (STM) and long-term memory (LTM).			

3

		3.7.3: STM and STSS: capacity, duration, encoding, chunking, selective attention.			
		3.7.4: LTM: capacity, duration, encoding, recall, multi-store memory.			
		3.7.5: Link between STSS, STM and LTM in terms of retrieval and rehearsal and how this affects output.			
		3.7.6: Measuring reaction and response times using appropriate technology. Hick's Law, simple/choice reaction time. Plotting, interpreting and analysing data generated from reaction and response times. Psychological refractory period. Implications to a coach and performer in optimising performance.			
		3.7.7: Understanding that schema theory is an organised package of information stored in LTM that updates and modifies motor programmes. Recall schema as in information about producing the movement. Recognition schema as in judging the movement. Schemas based on knowledge of the initial conditions, response specifications, sensory consequences and movement outcomes. Implications of schema theory to a coach and performer in optimising performance.			

COACHING STYLES

COMMAND

More of an **AUTHORITARIAN** approach to coaching, where learners must follow orders directly from the coach.

ADVANTAGES

- suit **novice** performers that need in-depth instruction
- helpful for big or hostile groups that need order
- useful where danger is present. **eg** throwing events in athletics (shot, javelin etc), ski-ing, rock climbing.
- where quick & hard decisions need to be made. **eg** in final time-out the coach will draw up a final play to try and get the win in a game of basketball.

DISADVANTAGES

- does not allow performers to express own ideas or to improve creativity within a performance.
- performers in the **autonomous stage** possess high levels of kinesthesis & would be able to use their own **intrinsic feedback** to adjust performance if required.

THERE ARE 4 MAIN

Styles for you to learn...

- **COMMAND**
- **RECIPROCAL**
- **GUIDED DISCOVERY**
- **PROBLEM-SOLVING**

COACHING STYLES

- The spectrum of teaching/coaching styles was **first** designed by Mosston & Ashworth (1994), with **11** teaching styles being suggested. This provided a framework & a guide for sports coaches & PE teachers.

TEACHING STYLE

A B C D E F G H I J

- Teacher Decision (blue)
- Pupil Decision (yellow)

- **Woods (1998)** identified that there were **4** main coaching styles (command, reciprocal, guided discovery & problem-solving).

- From the spectrum (above), you can see that if the style of coaching is close to **A**, then it will identify as more of a **COMMAND** style. The closer the coaching style to **J**, then the characteristics will be close to a **PROBLEM-SOLVING** style.

Coaching Styles II

Guided Discovery

Allows the coach to guide the performer(s) to explore & find the correct movement pattern or TACTIC by giving clues, thereby including the performer(s) in the decision making process.

eg a handball team are prompted on how they could manipulate a particular defensive pattern.

Advantages
- Promotes creativity.
- Effective for high level performers (autonomous stage).
- Improves motivation & cohesion.

Disadvantages
- Time consuming.
- Not as effective when working with large groups or in the cognitive stage.

Disadvantages
- A lot of the time there is no real right or wrong method, only what best suits a given scenario/time.
- For advanced performers only. (though can be used for others intermittently).

Problem-Solving

A problem or scenario is set by the coach. Learners have to solve this without any advice.

eg a boxer may be tasked with creating TACTICS & counter movements against a taller opponent with a longer reach, fighting southpaw style.

Reciprocal

The performers will be involved in the process of learning, allowing them to take responsibility for their development & to improve confidence.

In a sports setting, reciprocal teaching cards could be used.

eg these cards could demonstrate the correct technique of a skill (badminton drop shot). Performers then develop their own & others technique from the information.

Advantages
- Improves leadership qualities & a sense of belonging to a group by giving responsibilities to complete a task.
- Improves social interaction & communication.
- Helps develop intrinsic feedback.

Disadvantages
- The coach must ensure the correct information is being learnt & so may have to monitor progress initially.
- This style is better suited to performers in the associative stage of learning, rather than the cognitive stage (as needs greater instruction).

Advantages
- More suited to advanced learners/performers, as they possess wider knowledge of TACTICS & approaches.
- Used to mimic competitive scenarios, thereby applying the principle of specificity & can help develop long term performers Long Term Memory (LTM) stores.

THE DEVELOPMENT OF TACTICS & STRATEGIES

TRADITIONAL VIEW

... of teaching the fundamentals of sport, especially 'games' have been to ensure that there has been some mastery of motor skills first, followed by the progressive introduction of tactics & strategies

* eg football, rugby, netball

This fits more in line with the associative perspective of learning, where skills are perfected first, as opposed to the more holistic approach from the cognitivists views.

STRATEGIES

... are the general approaches teams or individuals have towards a competitive game/ event.

- These elements are discussed in advance in order for the team/individual to organise themselves.

TACTICS

... are adaptations or 'smaller steps' to the configuration or strategy of play.

- They are therefore an adaptation to the opposition.

EXAMPLE

In Rugby League, the STRATEGY could be to minimise the wide opportunities for the opposition, therefore a TACTIC that the team could deploy would be based around an 'umbrella' style defence, where the outside defensive players move up quickly ahead of the inside players to reduce the opportunity to pass the ball out wide, forcing them back into the middle.

YOU NEED

To be able to UNDERSTAND & EXPLAIN a variety of TACTICS used in both individual & team sports. Some eg's include ...

- formations in a football match.
- Offensive/attacking plays in basketball.
- Bowling combinations & variations in cricket.
- Tactical approach to the 1500m
  i.e. strong start, hang behind the front pod, overtake on the straights, kick round the top bend & a strong 80m finish.

FACTORS THAT AFFECT TACTICS

Could include ...

- weather/ environmental conditions
- Fitness levels
- Type of match
  (anxiety, motivation, confidence)
- Ability of performers (themselves & opposition).

SKILLS

- In order to establish faults within a performer's technique & lack of skill development, a skill can be broken down into **SUB-ROUTINES** for closer analysis (This may prove difficult for more continuous style skills eg. running). However **video analysis** & the use of **photographs/still images** can prove to be an effective method, especially when comparing with a (more) 'perfect model.'

SUB ROUTINES

- There are **3** main phases that make up the sub routines. These are...

PREPARATION
EXECUTION
RECOVERY

{ Technical components of each phase need to be mastered in order to achieve success in the performance of an identified skill.

DISSECTION OF A SKILL

DISSECTION

By breaking down a skill for analysis, coaches can identify specific biomechanical & technical strengths & weaknesses. They can compare their own qualitative evaluations in comparison to quantitative outcomes (as well as against elite models).

This in turn allows for a **strategy/strategies** to be devised in order to develop certain identified weaknesses.

EXAMPLE

Shoulder Turn 91°

Hip Turn 45°

Professional Golfer

Shoulder Turn 60°

Hip Turn 34°

High Handicap Golfer

The 2 sketches show one phase (**preparation**) regarding the analysis of the golf swing. The use of technology (here it would be GolfTec) allows coaches & trainers to gain in-depth knowledge of certain parameters surrounding shoulder & hip rotation.

There is a <u>clear</u> difference

✳ This section relates closely to component 4 of the spec & more specific detail on technical analysis is found in the **PDP** guide.

THE CLASSIFICATION OF SKILLS

GROSS/FINE MOTOR SKILLS

Skills can be distinguished based on the size of the muscle groups required to execute the actions.

GROSS MOTOR SKILLS

- Require the use of large muscle groups. However, they require less precision when compared to FINE motor skills. They are categorised by the fundamental motor skills that include... walking, running/jumping etc.
  eg. long jump in athletics.

FINE MOTOR SKILLS

- Require greater control of smaller muscle groups. Larger muscle groups may be involved, however it is the smaller muscle groups that are key to the effective execution of the skill.
- Therefore a high degree of precision & hand/eye co-ordination is involved. eg. the wrist/finger action when spin bowling in cricket.

FINE

- Intricate & precise movements
- Small muscle groups
- High levels of hand/eye co-ordination required.

GROSS

- large muscle movements
- Not very precise
- Fundamental movement patterns.

There are 4 CONTINUA to learn...
- Gross/Fine
- Internally/externally paced
- Discrete/serial/continuous
- Open/closed.

SKILL

- Skill can be defined or categorised in many ways. However, in this section we will focus on MOVEMENT skills or MOTOR skills.
- Many skills involve a combination of complex movements put together in a co-ordinated manner & many of the theories base these skills on CLASSIFICATION CONTINUA.
- In this way skills are placed on a CONTINUUM based on their relative contribution (though this has an aspect of subjectivity).

SKILL

- can be defined as a...
'learned action/behaviour with the intention of bringing about pre-determined results (with maximum certainty & minimum outlay of time/energy.'

THE CLASSIFICATION OF SKILLS II

OPEN / CLOSED SKILLS

OPEN SKILLS
- are directly affected by the environment in which they are performed. They need some type of adaptation to the skill each time (it is not performed in the exact same way twice due to unpredictable environmental factors. (see below)

CLOSED SKILLS
- are performed in a predictable environment & are performed in the same manner each time as the sequence of the movement has been pre-learnt & mastered
- eg shot putt, free throw in basketball.

ENVIRONMENTAL FACTORS
- could include wind speed, pitch conditions, opposition (positions). Need to rely on past experiences, knowledge & perceptual skills to analyse situation & execute skill properly. eg a drive in cricket against spin bowling.

OPEN
- Unpredictable environment
- High load information
- eg football

CLOSED
- Predictable environment
- Low load information
- eg golf

DISCRETE / SERIAL / CONTINUOUS SKILLS

DISCRETE MOTOR SKILLS
- are one distinct movement, with an identifiable beginning & end. Can be repeatable but there will be a completely new beginning & so a new skill.
- eg Conversion kick in rugby.

SERIAL MOTOR SKILLS
- several Discrete movement put together in a series / sequence. eg gymnastics floor routine, triple jump.

CONTINUOUS MOTOR SKILLS
- repetitive movements. No clear start / finish. Each flows into next. eg running

DISCRETE
- brief, well defined
- clear start & end
- single skills

SERIAL
- complex
- many discrete skills

CONTINUOUS
- no obvious beginning or end
- repeated

INTERNALLY / EXTERNALLY PACED

INTERNALLY PACED
- or SELF PACED skills are instigated by the performer as they control the timing of the performance.
- These skills are usually performed within a CLOSED ENVIRONMENT.
- eg a putt in golf, a discus throw.

EXTERNALLY PACED
- are those skills where the timing of performance (of the skill) is determined by an outside source. eg - an official or opponent
- These skills are usually performed in an OPEN ENVIRONMENT.
- eg - reacting to the starters gun or a service return in table tennis.

INTERNALLY (SELF)
- Performer controls rate
- Usually closed skills.

EXTERNALLY
- Environment controls rate (includes opposition)
- Usually open skills & includes reaction

TRANSFER OF SKILLS

RETROACTIVE TRANSFER

- Learning a new skill has an influence on a previously learnt skill. This can be **positive** or **negative**.

- **Positive** - the use of soft hands when catching in rounders can transfer to a better cushioning catch when receiving a pass in netball (rather than snatching at it).

- **Negative** - learning a lofted drive in cricket (more bottom hand needed) can be counter-productive when trying to play a drive along the ground (more top hand needed).

PROACTIVE TRANSFER

- The influence of one skill on a skill **yet to be learnt**.

- **eg.** once a motor programme has been developed for a forehand in tennis, this can be altered to develop into a top spin (same motor programme, but slightly modified technique).

ZERO TRANSFER

- Skills learnt from one sport have **no** impact of learning new skills in another sport.

- **eg.** perfecting a lofted pass technique in football has no impact on developing the butterfly stroke in swimming.

TRANSFER OF SKILLS

- refers to when skills have been developed in one situation & then can be used in others.

- It is important for teachers & coaches to develop the fundamental skills & then provide further challenge through different environments in order for performers to adapt or transfer the prior learning to a new situation.

POSITIVE TRANSFER

- Learning & performance of one skill is enhanced by the learning & performance of developing **another skill**.

- **eg.** being able to transfer weight, swing & hit a ball in baseball can have a positive influence in the development of batting skills in cricket.

NEGATIVE TRANSFER

- Learning & performance of a skill **interferes** with the learning of another skill.

- **eg.** even though the skills are similar, the techniques are different. Therefore, the wrist action required in badminton is different compared to tennis, where a rigid wrist action is required.

BILATERAL TRANSFER

- the transfer of a skill from **one limb to another**.

- **eg.** - learning to kick a football with both feet (left & right).

THE ASSOCIATIVE THEORIES

THE ASSOCIATIONIST OR CONNECTIONISTS

Perspective of learning refers to theories that relate to strengthening the stimulus-response bond (S-R bond).

This bond can be strengthened either by conditioning a response (classical conditioning) or by reinforcement (operant conditioning). Both methods allow for skills to further develop the long term memory.

CLASSICAL CONDITIONING

- Pavlov (1902) developed the theory of classical conditioning where his study of dogs salivating at the sound of a ringing bell could be conditioned ...

... hence strengthening the S-R bond.

- The association of food when the bell rang would ultimately lead to a conditioned response, which would become automatic.

- In sport, performers are conditioned to stop play when they hear the referees whistle.

- In addition, different cues in sport that a performer was trained (or been conditioned for), can lead to automatic responses. eg the twisting of hips in boxing can be a stimulus for the opponent to react to a punch that is about to be thrown, allowing the opponent to slip the punch, or counter-attack.

CLASSICAL CONDITIONING

Situation → Behaviour

Situation --- Consequence

↑ Repetition

Situation

Behaviour

Consequence

THE ASSOCIATIVE THEORIES II

OPERANT CONDITIONING

- Rewards & positive reinforcement can be given to performers as they progress through their sport.
- eg certificates for each stage of the swimming programme (5m, 10m, 25m etc), although teachers & coaches must be wary that the reward does not become more important than the enjoyment & the intrinsic value they get from performing/participating.

- However, if an action is wrong, then no reward (negative reinforcement) or a punishment is given, therefore weakening the S-R bond & the likelihood of this occurring would be minimal.

- Developed by Skinner (1944), operant conditioning involves manipulating & modifying behaviours through trial & error.

- The use of positive reinforcement & providing a reward helps to strengthen the S-R bond, as the action will be repeated.

OPERANT CONDITIONING

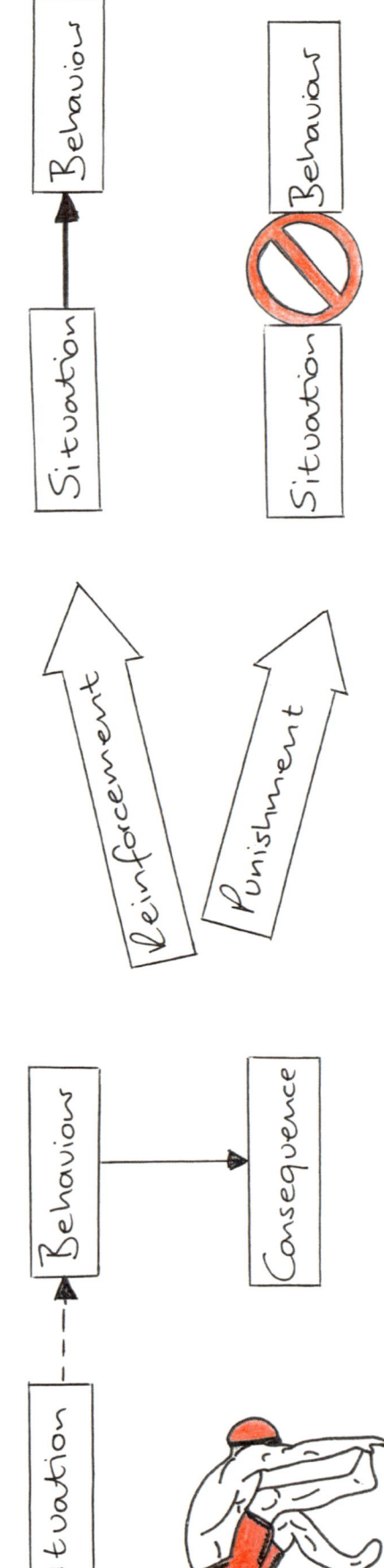

Situation → Behaviour

Situation ⊘ Behaviour

Reinforcement   Punishment

Situation ⤍ Behaviour → Consequence

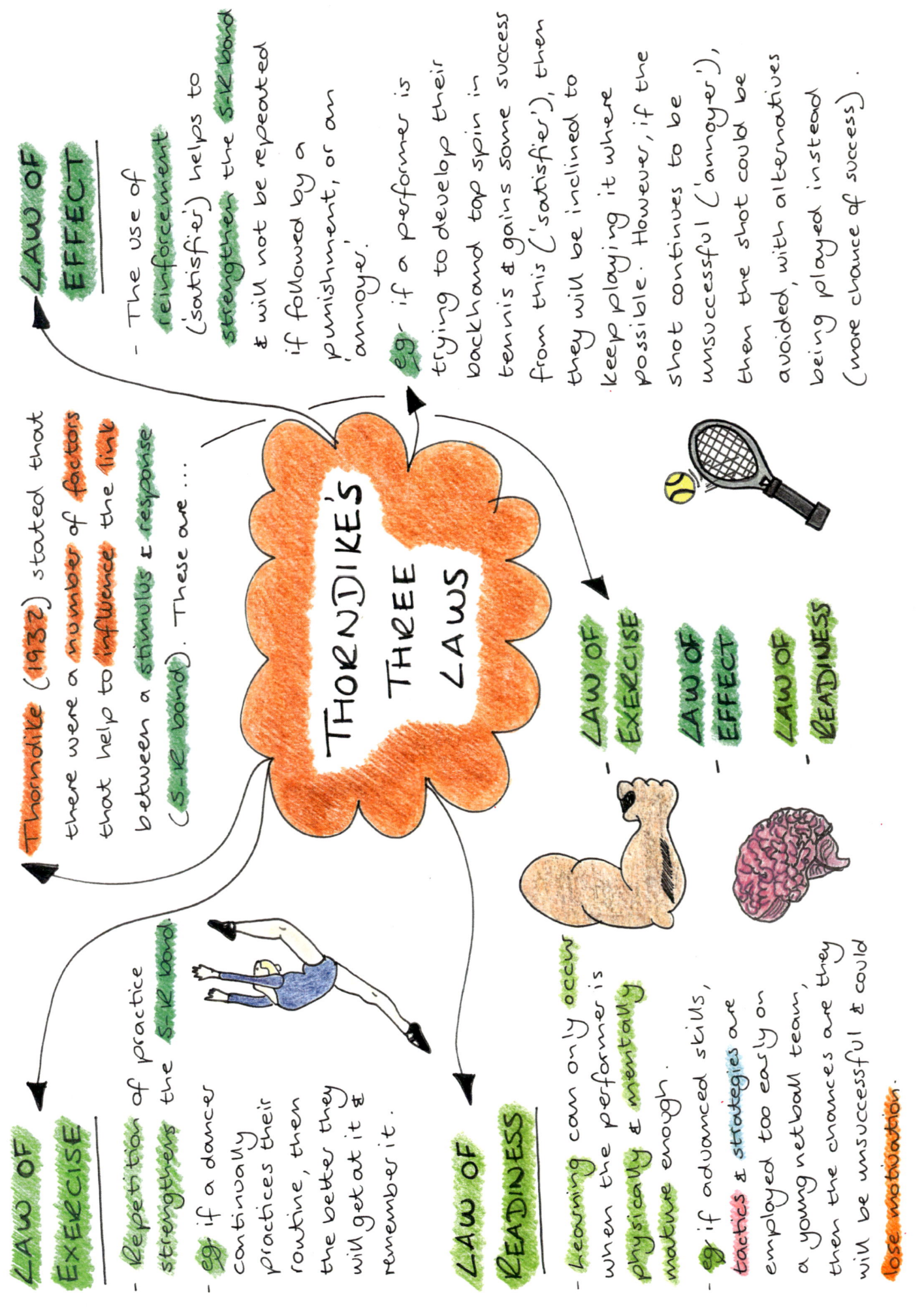

LAW OF EFFECT

- The use of reinforcement ('satisfier') helps to strengthen the S-R bond & will not be repeated if followed by a punishment, or an 'annoyer'.

- eg if a performer is trying to develop their backhand top spin in tennis & gains some success from this ('satisfier'), then they will be inclined to keep playing it where possible. However, if the shot continues to be unsuccessful ('annoyer'), then the shot could be avoided, with alternatives being played instead (more chance of success).

Thorndike (1932) stated that there were a number of factors that help to influence the link between a stimulus & response (S-R bond). These are...

THORNDIKE'S THREE LAWS

- LAW OF EXERCISE
- LAW OF EFFECT
- LAW OF READINESS

LAW OF EXERCISE

- Repetition of practice strengthens the S-R bond

- eg if a dancer continually practices their routine, then the better they will get at it & remember it.

LAW OF READINESS

- Learning can only occur when the performer is physically & mentally mature enough.

- eg if advanced skills, tactics & strategies are employed too early on a young netball team, then the chances are they will be unsuccessful & could lose motivation.

FITTS & POSNER'S THREE STAGES OF LEARNING

AUTONOMOUS

- This stage is sometimes called the **automatic phase** (the final stage).
- The performer exhibits **little or no conscious thought** into the execution of skills. He/she becomes **'highly proficient.'**
- This is more of an **elite stage**, where performers possess a **kinaesthetic feel** for their actions & generally **focus** more on **tactics & strategies**.
- Performers at this stage are better at **processing relevant** information, picking up on important cues & anticipating counter attacks.
- eg. an elite badminton player can anticipate a return shot by the position of the shuttle, the body angle of his/her opponent or movement pattern on court.

COGNITIVE

- The **early phase** (initial stage) of learning, where the fundamentals of a skill or performance are the main focus.
- It is categorised by **beginners** (or novice performers) using a **range of information** (mainly through demonstration) to form mental pictures that will help them to replicate the actions, if the demonstration has been shown correctly (otherwise may confuse and/or show incorrect technique).
- This phase requires a **lot of visual guidance & command style leadership/teaching.**

ASSOCIATIVE

- The **intermediate phase** (or practice stage) where performers are starting to develop fundamental skills to a more advanced level.
- A 'revisit' to the **cognitive phase** is typical in the early stages.
- Performers start to develop a **kinaesthetic feel** & will require further assistance via a combination of visual & verbal guidance from their coach.
- **focus** - eliminate small errors

STAGES

- Some performers may move through the stages quickly, or the skill is easy to learn. Some may be more complex & may never be learnt/reached.

- Fitts & Posner (1967) suggest that there are **specific stages of learning** & that this process is sequential.
- They identified **3 stages** & they are ...
  * links to **GUIDANCE** & **FEEDBACK**.

PRACTICE METHODS

Include...

PART PRACTICE

- Is effective when developing low organisational skills & complex skills, as it identifies sub-routines that performers can learn, practice & perfect before moving on to the next phase. Also helps develop serial skills & movements.

- eg. teaching a lay up in basketball. Performers will be able to develop their dribbling skills, then the pick-up & 2-step motion, the jump & then finally the shot itself.

- Advantages - Allows novice performers to gain confidence with each step, increasing the chance of success at different stages. (aids motivation). Also allows for improvements in areas of weakness.

- Disadvantages - The fluency of the skill is not learnt straight away & performers may lack the kinaesthetic feel to make faster progress.

PROGRESSIVE / PART PRACTICE

- Effective for developing serial skills (broken down into sub-routines). Once a sub-routine has been learnt, this is then linked with the next movement of a sequence.

- Effective for developing routines in gymnastics & dance.

PRACTICES

WHOLE - PART WHOLE PRACTICE

- Involves initial exposure to the whole skill before breaking it down into parts - then put back together.

- Particularly beneficial for serial & low organisational skills. Performers get a look at how it is performed & practice the whole skill before attempting the phases.

- Performers gain better kinaesthetic feel for the movement. eg lay-up.

PRACTICE

- The term 'practice makes perfect' is a term commonly used, however practice can only be of benefit to a performer if it is the right type or method.

- The type of 'appropriateness' of practice will then influence the effectiveness of skill development.

- Teachers, coaches, mentors will need to decide the best approach for the performers, though this will vary during a season (to account for improvements or to vary training).

WHOLE PRACTICE

- A skill is taught without breaking it down into sub-routines. Well suited to high organisational skills.

- Relevant for more advanced performers. They have the knowledge & skill level to execute the practice correctly. Allows performers to gain kinaesthetic feel for the whole movement (better fluency from practice to competition). Someno eg lofted pass in football. already developed for kicking, so just slight adjustments to technique using the whole method to develop the lofted pass.

16

DISTRIBUTED

- This allows the practice session to be broken down into different sections, focussing on various parts of a performance or skill(s) in one session.

- Ideally for novice performers that require more extensive feedback, performers with lower levels of conditioning, or for variety in a session that can work on an individual or team weaknesses.

- Distributed practice can also refer to several shorter training sessions throughout a week, rather than fewer & longer massed sessions.

- It is this type of practice that has found to be more effective in comparison to massed practice.

PRACTICE STRUCTURES

There are **4** main practice structures to learn. They are...

- MASSED PRACTICE
- DISTRIBUTED PRACTICE
- VARIABLE PRACTICE
- FIXED PRACTICE

MASSED

- Involves sessions of long duration with no breaks.

- Requires performers to be highly conditioned & of a 'more elite' standard, where they can rely on their own intrinsic feedback to help rectify any issues with performance.

- Allows 'more elite' performers to test their skills when fatigued.

- Only used during pre season or for endurance based events, such as long distance running, cycling & swimming.

VARIABLE

- Involves a variety of activities and/or situations to mimic a competitive situation. Allows performers to not only continue to develop the skill, but to gain exposure to performing it in a more challenging & everchanging environment.

- Is not only relevant for the development of open skills, but for 'more elite' performers (although coaches will slowly develop novice athletes into this type of practice to prepare for a more competitive environment)

FIXED

- Involves repetition of an activity so skills can be 'overlearnt', & to develop a specific motor programme.

- Ideal for skills performed in the same way in practice & competition. No variation due to the environment. - closed skills. eg golf putt, basketball free throw.

- Also used for novice performers in order to learn the fundamentals of the skill.

GUIDANCE

- Guidance helps to improve & optimise performance. Types of guidance are often used together. These are...
  - VERBAL & VISUAL
  - MANUAL & MECHANICAL

VISUAL

- This can be conducted through demonstration, video or visual aids (pictures, manuals, displays). Show the skill to the performer.
- Should be realistic & emphasise the skill to be learnt with correct technique. Incorrect technique will lead to confusion & a lack of progress in skill/technique development.
- Especially appropriate for performers in the cognitive stage of learning – allows them to gain a mental picture of the whole skill.
- eg video can be used to help demonstrate parts of a dance routine. Mental picture created & locate visual cues. (Dartfish, GolfTEC).

  + good for novices
  + good to see skill
  + quick

  ‒ may learn from incorrect demonstration
  ‒ questions?

VERBAL

- Is given when learning or practising a skill.
- You need to learn...
  - VERBAL
  - VISUAL
  - MANUAL
  - MECHANICAL

- often used in conjunction with visual guidance & used with more competent performers.
- eg provide key points of how to perform a push pass in hockey, which is then supported by a demonstration from the coach.
- Performers can be faced with information overload with verbal guidance, especially novice performers in the cognitive stage of learning.
- Why? They do not fully understand the technical points of a new skill.
- Performers in the autonomous stage of learning are able to cope with more verbal guidance, as they already understand the technical aspects, though during a competitive situation, key points only should be emphasised.
- Be concise & clear.

  + can make it detailed
  + quick
  + instructions in chunks

  ‒ cannot see
  ‒ hard to visualise
  ‒ language may be too complex
  ‒ talk for too long.

18

GUIDANCE

The different **TYPES** of guidance are best suited to performers at different **stages of learning**. The links are highlighted below...

MECHANICAL

- Use of mechanical aids to **control or restrict movements**.
- **eg** stabilisers on a bike, flotation devices/armbands when swimming, a harness in trampolining.
- Elite runners can also use **'assisted training'** where someone in front pulls them along to increase their running speed.
- Used to assist with safety, regulations & confidence.
- Can add some level of kinaesthesis, however a disadvantage could be that performers become **'over-reliant'** on these devices, reducing the level of intrinsic **feedback** & so the rate of progress is hampered.

+ reassures performer
+ reduces risk of injury
+ builds confidence

- un-natural feel
- performer becomes over reliant
- cost. can be very expensive.

MANUAL

- Physical support for either safety reasons, **eg** to assist a performer through difficult gymnastic vaulting sequence for the first time, or in order to teach a **new skill** with the correct technique, **eg** a coach **manually moving** a performer's arm into the correct position when playing a backhand in tennis.
- This can **assist/aid** with the performer's development of **kinaesthetic awareness** in the **cognitive stage** of learning. However, the performer **must** be given the opportunity **to develop** the skill on their own gradually (to fully develop their kinesthesis).

+ reassures performer
+ builds confidence
+ reduces risk of injury
+ beginners

- safeguarding issue?
- un-natural feel
- performer becomes reliant
- 1:1 needed.

LINKS WITH STAGES OF LEARNING

VISUAL - good for cognitive & associative stages, as can see what to do.

VERBAL - good for all stages. Very useful for **autonomous** (use if combined with visual. Cuse information easily).

MANUAL - good for all, especially **cognitive**.

MECHANICAL - especially good for beginners (cognitive) - reassure.

INTRINSIC

- Comes from the performer & kinaesthetic's...
- mainly through sensory feelings.
- As a result of this, intrinsic feedback is more effective as performers' improve in standard.
  ie elite performers
- Performers in the cognitive stage of learning have not fully developed their motor programmes & so their kinaesthetic awareness will not be at the appropriate level to provide intrinsic feedback.

FEEDBACK can take many, many different forms, including...

- POSITIVE
- INTRINSIC
- TERMINAL
- KNOWLEDGE OF RESULTS
- NEGATIVE
- EXTRINSIC
- CONCURRENT
- KNOWLEDGE OF PERFORMANCE

FEEDBACK

EXTRINSIC

- Comes from an external source eg. coach, peers, video etc.
- Is essential for novice performers that rely on 'more expert' advice that can also potentially aid motivation.
- However, this extrinsic feedback must be accurate, so should be given by an expert or qualified leader.
- The awareness of over-reliance on extrinsic feedback should also be considered.
- Why? Will hamper progress if they are always seeking external advice or approval.

FEEDBACK should be...

- Detailed but not too long.
- Specific.
- Given in age appropriate language (eg use of technical terms).
- Given ASAP (where appropriate).
- Relevant to the performer, not just generalised.
- Accurate.
- Constructive.

POSITIVE

- Constructive feedback that offers praise & encouragement.
- Usually external (extrinsic).
- Should outline what was performed correctly.
- eg after performing a sprint start in athletics, the coach may praise a young athlete about their good body position & balance.
- Important for novices/beginners, so they know what to repeat, as it also aids motivation.
- Coaches also need to be wary with too much positive feedback. If incorrect movements are praised it will reinforce inappropriate S-R bonds.

NEGATIVE

- feedback that is used to suppress an aspect of performance. Can be useful, but further feedback should follow on how to correct errors in technique.
- Regular negative feedback - demotivate.
- Useful for both beginners & experts. It is important when fine tuning technique (expert performer) eg feedback involving the slight change of body position in cycling to reduce drag.

FEEDBACK

KNOWLEDGE OF PERFORMANCE

- A form of extrinsic feedback where the performer gains an understanding about their performance in terms of form, technique & quality of an aspect of their performance.
- focus on areas of weakness, rather than overall outcome.
- More concerned with whether this targeted area was performed better than previously.
- Can form part of an athletes periodised training plan.
- eg a tennis player looking at developing their success rate on 1st serves early in the season.
- This type of feedback is also important for beginners, as the development of skill, technique & teamwork are more important at a younger age than just the outcome of a game.

KNOWLEDGE OF RESULTS

- However, knowledge of results in the form of how successful their technique was is important, as performers can link newly learnt technique with success.
- eg a younger netball GS will want to know if their shot has gone in after practicing their technique for an extended period of time.
- Knowledge of the outcome of performance, whether you were successful, or if you won or lost, form the basis for this type of feedback.
- Elite athletes will focus more on this (personal & final score).
- Younger & novice/beginner performers should avoid - focus on developing overall performance.

CONCURRENT

- Information a performer receives about their performance during the activity.
- Can be either intrinsic (elite performer, kinaesthetic feel regarding the execution of a skill), or extrinsic (from a coach for a novice performer, or through knowledge of results).
- A performer is able to make adjustments to their performance (if the game lasts long enough or more attempts possible).
- eg tennis player adjusting their service technique on the 2nd serve as they have detected an issue either intrinsically or verbally from a coach.
- The use of GPS data during a rugby match by the analysts to monitor work rate & used to base substitute decisions on.

TERMINAL

- Information a performer receives about their performance after the activity.
- Comes from an extrinsic source & can be straight after (high jumper looking at a big screen to view their technique), or extended time after (a video analysis of a rugby match early in the week after a game).

OPEN & CLOSED LOOP CONTROL

- The open & closed loop control theory explains how different skills are controlled by the brain
- Some skills are performed automatically (without conscious control), while others require more concentration.
- The brain selects an executive motor programme depending on the type of skill to be carried out. There are **3** levels of control...

LEVEL 2 - CLOSED LOOP

- Performer pays more attention to the requirements of the task.
- Feedback is internal/intrinsic & received through proprioception & kinesthesis from the muscles & not the brain.
- This allows for a short feedback loop.
- The brain can make an adjustment to the skill(s) that are not conscious during performance as a result of feedback that maintains fluency of movement.
- eg - continuous or ongoing movements that could include balancing body position during a kayaking slalom, or adjusting position in cycling when making slight changes in direction.

LEVEL 1 - OPEN LOOP

- Skills are performed subconsciously.
- Actions are linked to a person's memory trace & linked to the AUTONOMOUS stage of learning.
- The skill has been well learnt & is performed fast, as no time to adjust to any feedback.
- Skills are generally SIMPLE, SELF-PACED & performed in a CLOSED ENVIRONMENT
- eg tennis serve, golf swing, shot putt.

LEVEL 3 - CLOSED LOOP

- The performer is consciously creating the movements & adjusting the execution based on feedback received from the brain, therefore a longer feedback loop.
- The performance tends to be slower due to the amount of attention required to external (extrinsic) feedback.
- Relates to more novice/beginner performers, performing continuous or ongoing movements. eg passing a football, a shot in tennis.

Level 1 OPEN LOOP CONTROL
Executive Motor → Movement
Golf Swing

Level 2 CLOSED LOOP CONTROL
Executive Motor ↔ Movement
Balance in Gymnastics

Level 3 CLOSED LOOP CONTROL
Executive Motor ↔ Movement
Tennis Shot

Information Processing

Information Processing can be outlined by using this diagram...

```
INPUT → STIMULUS IDENTIFICATION → Response Selection → Response Programming → OUTPUT
```

Each of these steps or stages is explained in more detail in the relevant section on this page.

DCR Process

- In order to select the most relevant skill for a situation, the information must first be processed.
- This occurs through the **DETECTION, COMPARISON & RECOGNITION (DCR)** process.

INPUT

- Information is received from the environment via the **sensors** (sensory input).
- Vision, auditory & proprioception provide the majority of sensory input.

STIMULUS IDENTIFICATION

- Information is temporarily stored & the inputs that are seen to be relevant are stored in the short-term memory (**STM**).
- Detecting & interpreting any relevant information will lead to this being stored in the **STM**.
- eg. the performer will identify important cues from the environment, such as the flight / trajectory of the ball.

RESPONSE SELECTION

- The information is interpreted & compared with information within the **STM**, leading to a decision on what action is to be undertaken.
- eg. catch the ball

RESPONSE PROGRAMMING

- Instructions are sent out to the muscles (via the nervous system), to perform the skill.

OUTPUT

- The action is carried out.
- **Feedback** is stored for future reference.

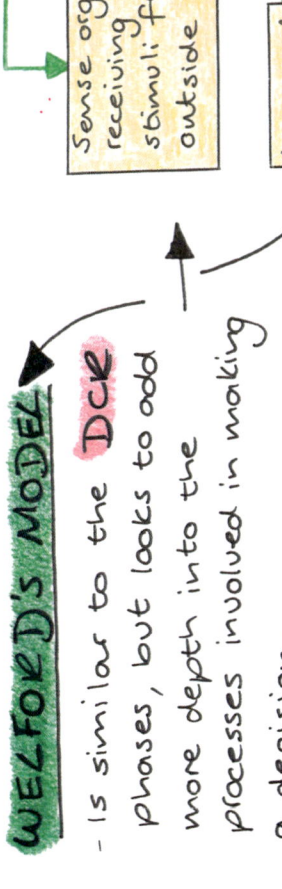

Welford's Model flowchart:

Sense organs receiving stimuli from outside → Perception

Internal sensors → Perception

Perception → Short term store → Decision making → Effector control → Effectors

Long term store

WELFORD'S MODEL
- Is similar to the DCR phases, but looks to add more depth into the processes involved in making a decision.

DISPLAY
- A large range of stimuli are detected from the environment through the senses.

PERCEPTUAL MECHANISMS
- The information received from the senses is organised (relevant & irrelevant) & anything perceived as important is sent to the STM. Those that are not are forgotten.
- This perception stage is more efficient for an elite performer (when compared to a novice/beginner) due to past experiences.
- They are able to use SELECTIVE ATTENTION with more accuracy. Aids making quick & correct decisions.

DECISION MECHANISM
- A decision is made by comparing relevant information with previous experiences in the long-term memory (LTM) store.
- The decision will influence future decisions & perception.

EFFECTOR MECHANISM
- The brain will then send a message to the body (limbs/muscles) via the nervous system with instructions to carry out the movement.

EFFECTORS/MUSCULAR SYSTEM
- Movement carried out.

FEEDBACK

INTRINSIC - mainly via proprioceptors. Inform the brain of movement outcome.

EXTRINSIC - from various sources (coaches, peers, KoR). Inform you of the outcome.

* Actions/results then stored for future & process repeats itself.

WHITING'S MODEL

Legend:
- Effector Mechanisms
- Musculas System
- Output Data
- Feedback Data

Body Boundary

- Selective Attention
- Translatory Mechanisms
- Perceptual Mechanisms
- Receptor Systems

Input Data from Display

WHITING'S MODEL

- Looks to explain how the performer can deal with a vast amount of information from the surroundings, process it & then make quick & correct decisions.

- It is important that you can relate this to a sporting example (shown in each stage).

INPUT DISPLAY

- The performer will acknowledge the movement/action. eg your opponent has played a return shot (in tennis).

RECEPTOR SYSTEMS

- Like with Welford's model, a large amount/range of stimuli are detected from the environment through the senses. eg track the trajectory of a ball.

PERCEPTUAL MECHANISM

- The part of the brain which perceives the surroundings & gives them meaning. eg see & hear relevant movements from the surroundings.

TRANSLATORY MECHANISM

- The part of the brain where decisions are made & is translated from the information provided & compared to previous experiences. eg the ball is going to land on your right hand side & bounce waist height.

EFFECTOR MECHANISM

- Motor programme is used & impulses are sent via the nervous system to the relevant muscles to carry out the actions. eg relevant motor units activated to carry out a forehand return.

MUSCULAR SYSTEM

- The muscles carry out the relevant response (contract). eg execute forehand shot.

OUTPUT

- The effector mechanism & muscle movement are complete. eg forehand shot has been played.

FEEDBACK

- When the motor programme has been put into action, new information is created. If successful, it will strengthen the motor programme.

- Can be INTRINSIC (senses, proprioception) and/or EXTRINSIC (coaches, peers, visual playback).

THE THREE MEMORY SYSTEMS

SHORT-TERM MEMORY

- Is sometimes called the working memory, receiving information from the senses (mainly via auditory senses) & decides WHAT information is sent to the LTM.

- The STM can store between 5-9 items at a time for up to 30 seconds.

- CHUNKING information, that is grouping actions together as opposed to remembering long strings of information, can also be used to enhance memory.

- Information from the STM is transferred to the LTM only if the information is rehearsed or repeated & is deemed important.

- This process is called ENCODING.

- The STM requests motor programmes from the LTM that is then retrieved & DECODED in order for the correct movement pattern to be executed.

The 3 to learn are ...
- SHORT-TERM SENSORY STORES (STSS)
- SHORT-TERM MEMORY (STM)
- LONG TERM MEMORY (LTM)
-

SHORT-TERM SENSORY STORES

- Information is received through a wide range of senses or stimuli from the environment.

- There is a very large capacity to store this information, though it is temporary with a time-frame of ¼ - 1 second.

- These stores filter information through SELECTIVE ATTENTION. Relevant information is filtered through to the STM & information that is deemed unimportant is lost, forgotten & replaced.

- This is important for the development of sporting performance as important cues are remembered.

- Reaction time & the retrieving of appropriate information regarding the execution of skills can be enhanced through the development of selective attention.

LONG-TERM MEMORY

- The LTM has infinite capacity & stores information indefinitely. This explains why you never forget how to ride a bike!

- Information held has been well learnt or overlearnt & practiced, allowing the performer to apply the skill in an automatic (autonomous) way.

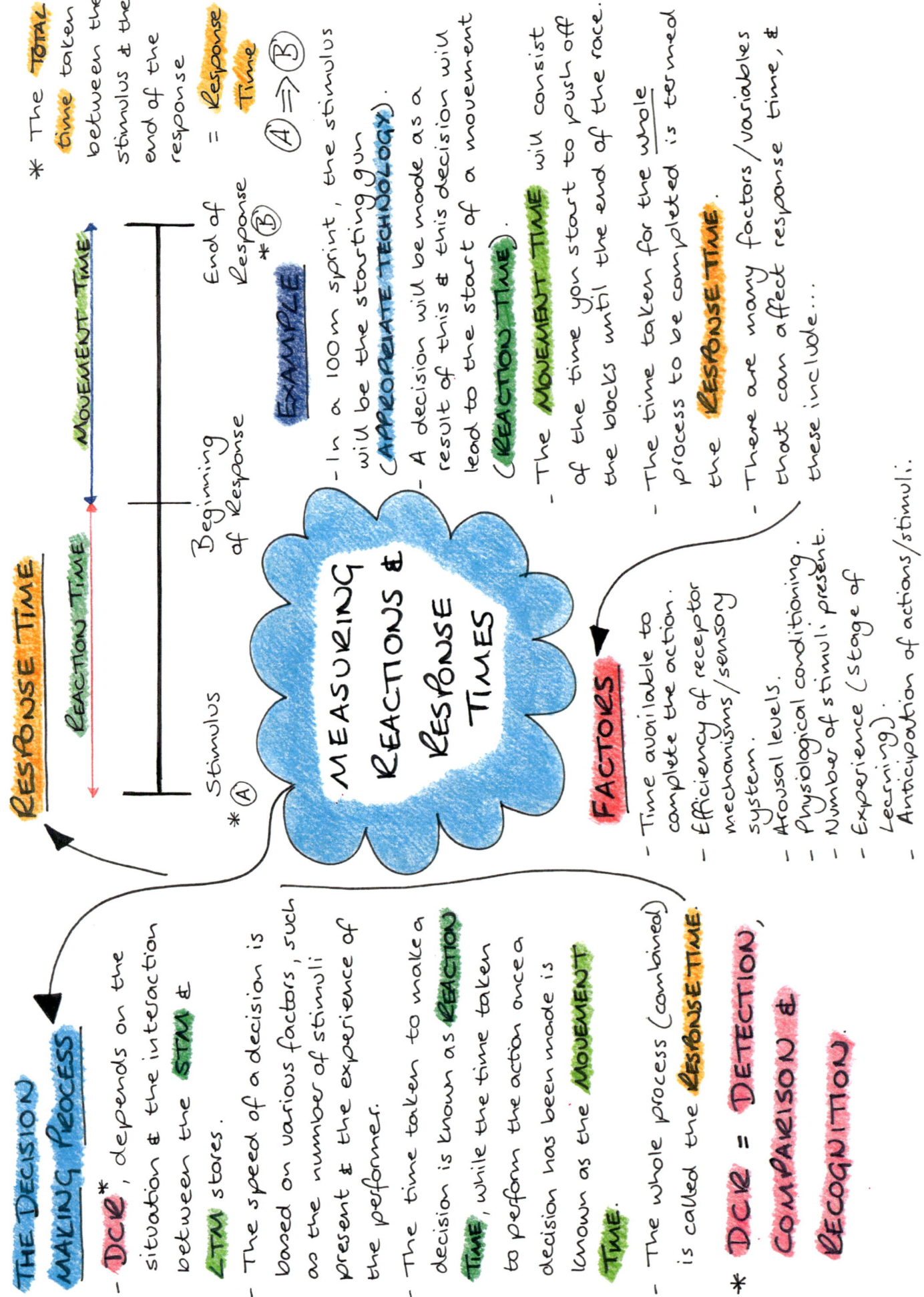

* The **TOTAL** **time** taken between the stimulus & the end of the response

= Response Time

(A) ⇒ (B)

RESPONSE TIME

REACTION TIME | **MOVEMENT TIME**

Stimulus *(A)

Beginning of Response

End of Response *(B)

MEASURING REACTIONS & RESPONSE TIMES

EXAMPLE

- In a 100m sprint, the stimulus will be the starting gun (**APPROPRIATE TECHNOLOGY**).
- A decision will be made as a result of this & this decision will lead to the start of a movement (**REACTION TIME**).
- The **MOVEMENT TIME** will consist of the time you start to push off the blocks until the end of the race.
- The time taken for the whole process to be completed is termed the **RESPONSE TIME**.
- There are many factors/variables that can affect response time, & these include...

FACTORS

- Time available to complete the action.
- Efficiency of receptor mechanisms/sensory system.
- Arousal levels.
- Physiological conditioning.
- Number of stimuli present.
- Experience (stage of Learning).
- Anticipation of actions/stimuli.

THE DECISION MAKING PROCESS

- **DCR***, depends on the situation & the interaction between the **STM** & **LTM** stores.
- The speed of a decision is based on various factors, such as the number of stimuli present & the experience of the performer.
- The time taken to make a decision is known as **REACTION Time**, while the time taken to perform the action once a decision has been made is known as the **MOVEMENT TIME**.
- The whole process (combined) is called the **RESPONSE TIME**.

* **DCR** = **DETECTION**, **COMPARISON** & **RECOGNITION**.

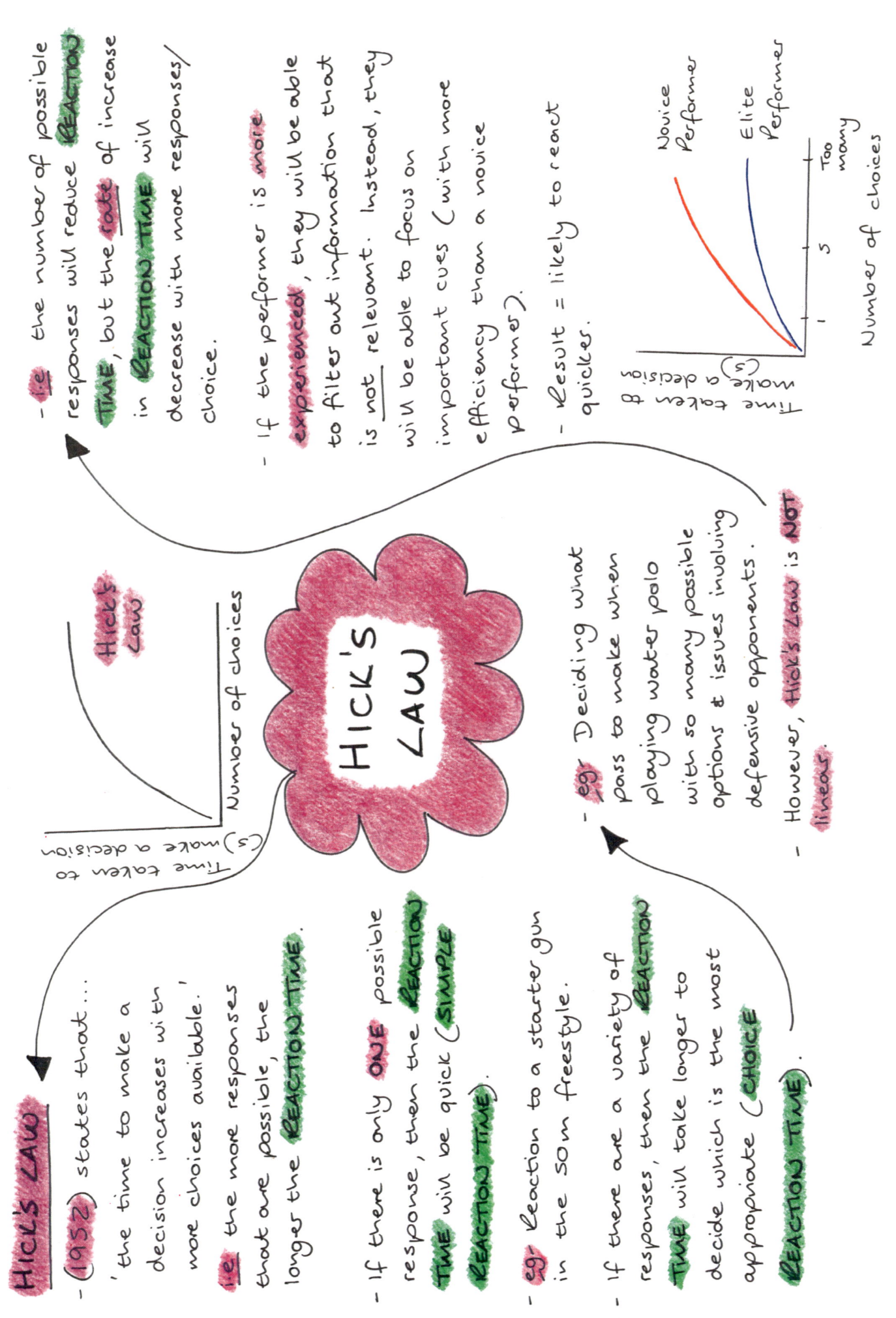

HICK'S LAW

HICK'S LAW
- (1952) states that...
'the time to make a decision increases with more choices available.'
- i.e the more responses that are possible, the longer the REACTION TIME.

- If there is only ONE possible response, then the REACTION TIME will be quick (SIMPLE REACTION TIME).
- eg. Reaction to a starter gun in the 50m freestyle.

- If there are a variety of responses, then the REACTION TIME will take longer to decide which is the most appropriate (CHOICE REACTION TIME).

- eg. Deciding what pass to make when playing water polo with so many possible options & issues involving defensive opponents.

- However, Hick's Law is NOT linear.

- i.e the number of possible REACTION responses will reduce responses will reduce, but the rate of increase in REACTION TIME will decrease with more responses/choice.

- If the performer is more experienced, they will be able to filter out information that is not relevant. Instead, they will be able to focus on important cues (with more efficiency than a novice performer).

- Result = likely to react quicker.

Hick's Law

Number of choices

Time taken to make a decision (s)

Time taken to make a decision (s)

Number of choices

Novice Performer

Elite Performer

1   5   Too many

STIMULUS ONE   STIMULUS TWO   RESPONSE ONE   RESPONSE TWO

PRP

PSYCHOLOGICAL REFRACTORY PERIOD

REFERS TO

- the period of time it takes to respond to a second stimulus after already being presented with the first stimulus.

- The **SINGLE CHANNEL HYPOTHESIS** states, that only **ONE** stimulus can be processed at any given time.

- Therefore only **ONE** decision & response can occurs.

- Once the process for one decision has started, it **must** be finished **before** processing the next stimulus. (See diagram).

- That is why it is so hard to defend a side-step in rugby, a step-over in football or adjust properly to a deflection (in any sport!)

- With regards to the deflection, that is why it is good **sporting etiquette** to raise your hand in apology when the ball hits the net & lands just over in tennis, as the opponent would already have processed the information & anticipated where the shot would have landed.

STRATEGIES TO REDUCE RESPONSE TIME

- Practice / build experiences to help shorten processing time & enhance anticipation

- Practice detecting relevant cues / real life sporting practices (replicating game play).

- Warm up physiological & psychological responses (eg - optimal arousal levels).

- Mental rehearsal / improve attention & focus.

- Improve fitness levels.

29

STRATEGIES TO DEVELOP SCHEMA

- Varied practice conditions so performers experience different situations & make it specific & relevant to the game or activity.

- The concept of transfer of skills is supported by schema.

- Feedback is important in order to update/correct a schema.

- Tasks should be challenging/gradually get more difficult.

- Slow motion practice methods to perfect motor movements.

- Chunk information to strengthen the STM & LTM memory - chaining, link actions & movements together.

- Mental rehearsal.

- Make learning meaningful. As a result, the performer is much more likely to remember it.

ADAPTING THE SCHEMA THEORY

RECALL SCHEMA - takes in important information *prior* to an action. Takes into account...

- **Initial conditions** - the knowledge of the environment. *eg.* conditions, surface, position of players.

- **Response specifications** - level of power, force, speed needed to complete the task - pass, shot etc.

SCHEMA THEORY

RECOGNITION SCHEMA - occurs during/after the performance of a skill to correct/alter a response for the future.

Takes into account...

- **Sensory consequences** - knowledge of performance gathered from sensory system feedback (kinaesthetic feel).

- **Movement outcomes** - knowledge of results, where the end result & comparison is made with the intended outcome (real to intended) Updates memory store for future reference if similar situation occurs again.

SCHEMA THEORY

- Schmidt (1975) suggested that the learning of skills was more of a cognitive function, rather than strengthening a response to a stimulus.

- This means we learn a number of generalised motor programmes, or **SCHEMA** that are adapted to differing sporting requirements.

MOTOR PROGRAMMES

- Are stored in the LTM & are strengthened through continued rehearsal, especially if it mimics real life scenarios.

- They are retrieved by comparing the recognised information with previous experiences.

- However, the LTM isn't large enough to store every single motor programme, hence the creation of **SCHEMAS**.

- This explains WHY sports performers can undertake many of the actions required (for their sport), with little conscious control.

- The LTM stores fewer motor programmes as movements can be mimicked & adjusted by running a SCHEMA.

Topic 3: Skill Acquisition

1. Give reasons as to why performers or teams will change their tactics in-between competitions and/or games. **(3 marks)**

2. Explain the difference between guided discovery and problem-solving coaching styles. **(4 marks)**

3. Define the following terms:
    a. Externally-paced skill **(1 mark)**
    b. Serial skill **(1 mark)**
    c. Continuous skill **(1 mark)**

4. Analyse how different skills within team games can be classified differently on the continua. **(8 marks)**

5. Some skills learnt in one activity can have an influence on the learning of skills in another.
    i) Define 'positive transfer of learning' with a relevant sporting example. **(2 marks)**
    ii) Outline how a coach can ensure the positive transfer of a skill. **(3 marks)**

6. Using sporting examples, describe the difference between proactive and retroactive transfer of skills. **(4 marks)**

7. The associative perspective of learning refers to theories that relate to strengthening the stimulus-response bond (S-R bond).
    a. Describe the difference between classical and operant conditioning. **(2 marks)**

b. **Outline** how a coach can use classical conditioning to develop sporting skills?

(2 marks)

c. **Explain** how positive and negative reinforcement can be used to develop the learning of sporting skills.

(4 marks)

8. **Describe** the different characteristics of each stage of Fitts and Posner's stages of learning.

(6 marks)

9. **Evaluate** the effectiveness of the different practice methods on development of sporting performance.

(8 marks)

10. **Explain** why a coach may choose to use a distributed practice structure as opposed to massed practice.

(6 marks)

11. **Analyse** the effectiveness of verbal and visual guidance in developing a new skill to a performer in the cognitive stage of learning.

(8 marks)

12. Using a specific example, **explain** how technology can be used as a guidance method to monitor and/or evaluate a performer in order to optimise success in sport.

(4 marks)

13. **Explain** when concurrent feedback and terminal feedback would be more appropriate to use in a sporting context.

(4 marks)

14. Using examples, **explain** the differences between the open loop control and closed loop control systems.

(4 marks)

15. **Explain** how the psychological refractory period occurs in team games.

(3 marks)

16. **Explain** the difference between recall schema and recognition schema.

(6 marks)

Total Marks: /87

Topic 4: Sport Psychology

What you need to learn:		Yes	Nearly	No
4.1: Factors that can influence an individual in physical activities	4.1.1: Knowledge and understanding of different personality theories and their application to different sporting situations. **Personality theories:** Trait (Innate) theory — introvert/extrovert, neurotic/stable (Eysenck, Cattell's 16 Personality Factors) Interactionist theory: Behaviour = function (personality, environment) Hollander's and Martens personality structure.			
	4.1.2: Wood's Triadic Model: ideas/cognitions, emotions/effects and actions/behaviour. Understanding how attitudes are formed and shape behaviour. Changing attitudes: negative to positive — create 'cognitive dissonance' — Festinger.			
	4.1.3: Arousal and its effect on performance. Positive/negative effects, under-/over-arousal, introverts/extroverts. Arousal and achieving optimal levels for performance — task differences, e.g. simple/gross skills, situational factors, stage of learning and personalities — Inverted-U hypothesis, Hull's Drive Theory. Catastrophe Theory.			
	4.1.4: Anxiety and its effect on performance. The three dimensions of anxiety: cognitive, somatic and behavioural. **Types of anxiety:** state and trait			

	anxiety. The effects of anxiety of performance: over arousal, choking and catastrophe theory. Relationship between arousal and anxiety. Stress and stressors leading to anxiety- physiological, psychological, behavioural symptoms. **Cognitive/Somatic strategies:** mental practice/rehearsal, use of visualisation and imagery, 'self talk', pre-game routines, relaxation techniques, centring, thought stopping, PMR (Progressive Muscle Relaxation).			
	4.1.5: Aggression v Assertion. Knowledge and understanding, in relation to the player, coach and spectator, of aggression and assertion and the difference between the two. **Theories:** - Instinct (Lorenz) - Social Learning (Bandura) - Aggressive-Cue Hypotheses (Berkowitz) - Frustration-Aggression Hypothesis (Dollard). **Types of aggression:** - Hostile - Channelled - Reactive - Instrumental Causes of aggression, e.g. over-arousal, under developed moral reasoning, bracketed morality,			

		and application to specific sporting situations. Strategies to reduce aggression/aggressive play.			
		4.1.6: Knowledge and understanding of motivation. **Types of motivation** — self-motivation characteristics, positive, negative, intrinsic and extrinsic; link to rewards — internal/external, tangible/intangible. **Theories of motivation:** • Achievement Motivation Theory (Atkinson and McClelland). • NAF (Need to Avoid Failure) and NACH (Need to Achieve). Characteristics of each and how they may be reflected in the same individual but in different circumstances and/or times. An application of these theories to optimise performance. Factors that influence behaviour: situation, personality, motivation and expectation. Use of goal setting to develop and enhance motivation.			
		4.1.7: Definition, knowledge and understanding of social facilitation, including social inhibition. The positive and negative effects on a performer. The role of and effect of 'others' — passive (audience/co-actors) — interactive others (competitors/spectators The effects of social facilitation on a novice			

	to a highly skilled performer, the dominant response and the link to arousal (Drive theory and Inverted-U). Causes of and the effects of Evaluation Apprehension (Zajonc and Cottrell). External influences, e.g. significant others, homefield advantage, distraction effect, proximity effect, and their impact on performance. Strategies to combat social inhibition.			
4.2: Dynamics of a group/ team and how they can influence the performance of an individual and/or team	4.2.1: Knowledge and understanding of the characteristics of a successful and cohesive group/team. Understanding that group cohesion is based on a combination of task or social cohesion. Theories Carron: the four factors that affect formation and development of a cohesive group/team — environmental, personal, leadership and team factors. Steiner: actual productivity = group productivity — losses due to faulty processes. Group dynamics and how they can influence the performance of an individual and/or team. Social loafing: causes and factors that contribute to minimising its effect. Coordination/cooperation factors: Ringelmann Effect. Strategies to develop group cohesion.			
4.3: Goal setting	4.3.1: Knowledge and understanding of SMART(ER) targets (specific, measurable,			

	achievable, realistic, time-bound, evaluated and recorded). The importance and relevance of goal setting and the different types used to optimise performance: subjective, objective, outcome/product, performance, process, realistic and aspirational goals; short-, medium- and long-term goals			
4.4: Attribution theory	4.4.1: A knowledge and understanding of reasons for success and failure in sport. Weiner's attribution theory and the four attributions: ability, effort, luck, task difficulty. The three main dimensions of attribution: locus of causality, locus of stability and locus of controllability. Strategies to allow for attribution retraining.			
4.5: Confidence and self-efficacy	4.5.1: Knowledge and understanding of self-confidence. Knowledge and understanding of Vealey's model of sport-specific confidence, including relevant sporting examples.			
	4.5.2: Self-efficacy Bandura Self-Efficacy: Explanation and effect of the four factors that build sport-specific self-confidence: past accomplishments, verbal persuasion, emotional arousal and vicarious experiences (modelling). Learned helplessness and its impact on performance.			

| 4.6: Leadership | 4.6.1: Knowledge and understanding of the importance of effective leadership and its impact on performance. The different types of leadership styles: autocratic, laissez-faire and democratic, based on the models of Fiedler and Chelladuri. Advantages and disadvantages of each leadership style. **Theories of leadership:** An understanding of how leaders are created: Trait theory (Great Man Theory) vs Social learning, Interactionist theory. | | | 38 |

TRAIT THEORY

- Trait theories see personality as being **innate** (born with) & that it is stable & predictable in **all** situations.

- It is **heredity** & passed on through genes.

- This means that **behaviour is easier to predict in all situations**, with the environment & the situation not playing much part in affecting **personality**.

- eg - a players **personality will not change** if it is a regular season game or play-off final.

- The **drawback** to the trait theory of personality is that the **environment & learning situations are not taken into account & that behaviour is not always predictable**.

HOLLANDER (1971)
defined personality as a 'combination of all the characteristics that make a person unique.'

PERSONALITY THEORIES

Focus on...

- **EYSENCK** (1975)
- **CATTELL** (1957)
- **HOLLANDER** (1971)
- **MARTENS**

PERSONALITY

... refers to individual differences in characteristic patterns of ...

- thinking
- feeling
- behaving.

- No **2** people have **exactly** the same type of personality.

- People behave in different ways in relation to various circumstances, reflecting an individual's most prominent characteristics, highlighting greater importance of personality traits in sport.

39

EYSENCK

... identified 4 primary personality traits or types.

- They are ...
  - **EXTROVERT**
  - **INTROVERT**
  - **STABLE**
  - **UNSTABLE**

- One way of explaining the extrovert/introvert continuum is based on Eysenck's work.

He argues that the difference between extroverts & introverts is because extroverts inherit an 'under aroused' nervous system & therefore seek extra stimulation.

- More specifically, part of the brain called the Reticular Activating System (RAS) can determine whether an athlete is more inclined to be an extrovert or an introvert.

UNSTABLE

EXTROVERT
- Tough
- Aggressive
- Excitable
- Impulsive
- Active
- Sociable
- Outgoing
- Responsive
- Lively
- Leader

INTROVERT
- Moody
- Rigid
- Unsociable
- Pessimist
- Quiet
- Passive
- Thoughtful
- Controlled
- Reliable
- Calm

STABLE

EXTROVERTS

- Crave excitement & take risks.
- Become bored easily.
- Tend to perform better with higher arousal levels.
- Extroverts prefer activities that involve gross motor skills, so team games are more favourable.
- Continuous/endurance activities (eg marathon running) are less appealing.

INTROVERTS

- Quiet & reserved.
- Already 'over aroused', so do not seek extra stimulation.
- Introverts prefer to take part in activities that require more precision (eg archery). Fine motor skills.

UNSTABLE

- or NEUROTIC personality traits are changeable, varied & so behaviour is unpredictable.
- eg a performer's mood can swing from situation to situation & suffer from higher levels of stress.

STABLE

- Are unchangeable, consistent & so behaviour is predictable.
- eg if a tennis player generally possesses less anxiety in a particular situation, they will then possess lower levels of anxiety in all situations.

CATTELL'S TRAIT THEORY (1957)

- According to Cattell, there is a **hierarchy of personality traits**.

- From previous studies he was able to apply factor analysis to reduce 171 characteristics to 16 key **personality factors**.

- Cattell believed that there was a continuum of **personality traits** & that each person contained all of these 16 traits, to a certain & variable degree. i.e high in some people but low in others.

- These **personality traits** were either ....

  SOURCE TRAITS or **SURFACE TRAITS**.

CATTELL

The **SOURCE TRAITS** are the 16 factors (left column).

The **SURFACE TRAITS** are the low score & high score columns.

These are the traits on the continuum.

SOURCE TRAITS
- The most important & found at the top of the continuum.

SURFACE TRAITS
- Influence behaviours at different intensities & regularity.

Factor	Low Score	High Score
Warmth	Cold, Selfish	Supportive, Comforting
Intellect	Instinctive, Unstable	Cerebral, Analytical
Emotional stability	Irritable, Moody	Level-headed, Calm
Aggressiveness	Modest, Docile	Controlling, Tough
Liveliness	Somber, Restrained	Wild, Fun-loving
Dutifulness	Untraditional, Rebellious	Conforming, Traditional
Social Assertiveness	Shy, Withdrawn	Uninhibited, Bold
Sensitivity	Coarse, Tough	Touchy, Soft
Paranoia	Trusting, Easy-going	Wary, Suspicious
Abstractness	Practical, Regular	Strange, Imaginative
Introversion	Open, Friendly	Private, Quiet
Anxiety	Confident, Self-assured	Fearful, Self-doubting
Open-mindedness	Closeminded, Set-in-ways	Curious, Exploratory
Independence	Outgoing, Social	Loner, Craves solitude
Perfectionism	Disorganised, Messy	Orderly, Thorough
Tension	Relaxed, Cool	Stressed, Unsatisfied

HOLLANDER'S (1971) PERSONALITY STRUCTURE

- States the structure has 3 layers:

PSYCHOLOGICAL CORE

- Basic attitudes & values that remain relatively constant.
- Influences responses.

TYPICAL RESPONSE

- the way someone responds to any given situation.
- based on the performers attitudes & beliefs (psychological core)
- eg cricketer 'walking' when out as reflects good etiquette & sportsmanship / fairplay.

ROLE - RELATED BEHAVIOUR

- Behaviour is influenced by the situation or environment/have
- May be totally different/have no resemblance to the psychological core (depending on strength of the pressures in the environment.
- eg a player may have to adjust to suit their new role. i.e team leader / captain.

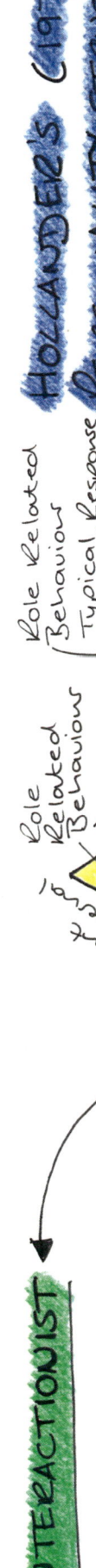

Role Related Behaviour
Typical response
Psychological Core

Role Related Behaviour
Social Environment
Dynamic
Constant
Typical Response
Psychological Core
Social Environment
Internal

INTERACTIONIST PERSPECTIVE

INTERACTIONIST

- This perspective suggests that we behave as a result of our innate core personality (genetic traits) & as a result of the environment (social learning).

- Interactionists see BEHAVIOUR (B) as being a FUNCTION (f) of both PERSONALITY (P) & the ENVIRONMENT (e).

- This therefore equates to ...

$$B = f (P.e)$$

or

$$B = f (P \times e)$$

- This explains how a rugby player may be quite shy & reserved off the pitch, but their behaviour changes to assertive & confontational on it.

MARTENS PERSONALITY STRUCTURE

- Is similar to Hollanders, though it looks to emphasise that role-related behaviour is very dynamic & dependent on the external social dynamic.

- The internal & consistent factors depend on the core traits of the performer. i.e do they have the 'will to win' & desire to achieve their goal, or are they more likely to give up & quit!?.

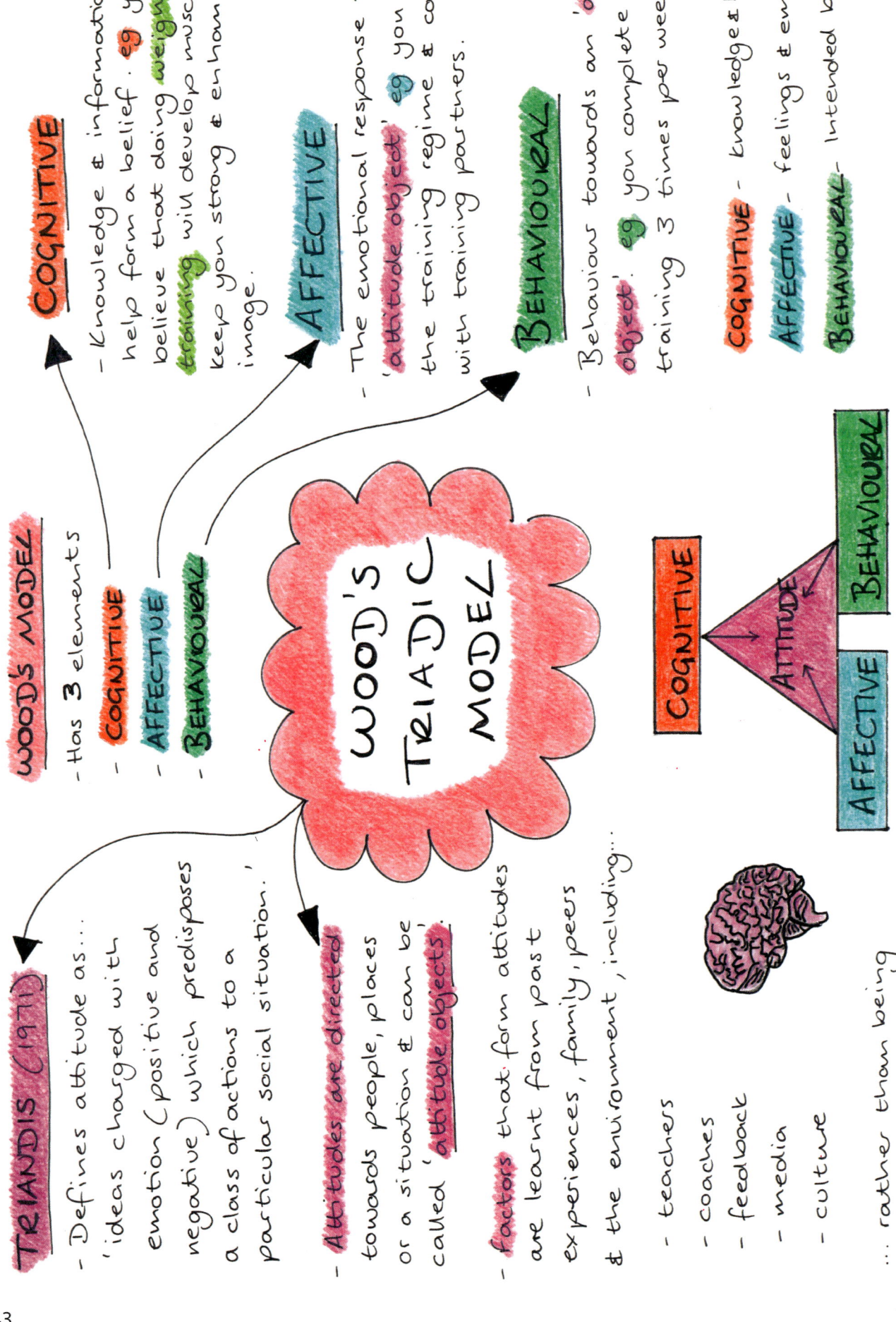

WOOD'S TRIADIC MODEL

WOOD'S MODEL
- Has 3 elements
  - COGNITIVE
  - AFFECTIVE
  - BEHAVIOURAL

COGNITIVE
- Knowledge & information help form a belief. eg you believe that doing weight training will develop muscle tone, keep you strong & enhance body image.

AFFECTIVE
- The emotional response to an 'attitude object'. eg you enjoy the training regime & competing with training partners.

BEHAVIOURAL
- Behaviours towards an 'attitude object'. eg you complete weight training 3 times per week.

COGNITIVE - knowledge & beliefs
AFFECTIVE - feelings & emotions
BEHAVIOURAL - intended behaviour

COGNITIVE

ATTITUDE

AFFECTIVE

BEHAVIOURAL

TRIANDIS (1971)
- Defines attitude as... 'ideas charged with emotion (positive and negative) which predisposes a class of actions to a particular social situation.'

- Attitudes are directed towards people, places or a situation & can be called 'attitude objects'.

- Factors that form attitudes are learnt from past experiences, family, peers & the environment, including...
  - teachers
  - coaches
  - feedback
  - media
  - culture

... rather than being innate (born with).

ATTITUDES AND BEHAVIOUR

PREJUDICE

- An extreme or strongly held attitude that is resistant to change, held previous to a direct experience.

- If an attitude is based on false information & is unfair, then this becomes a PREJUDICE (extreme attitude towards a person/situation.

PREJUDICE = to 'pre-judge'.

- PRE-JUDGING a person can lead to a certain expectancy of behaviour leading to...

STEREOTYPING (general inclination to place a person in categories according to an easy & identifiable set of characteristics).

STEREOTYPING

- Is rarely accurate but very resistant to change.

- eg's include...
- Boys are more competitive than girls.
- Black people are not very good at swimming.
- White people are not very good at 'explosive' sports'
 ... White Men Can't Jump!

METHODS OF ATTITUDE CHANGE

- Sports professionals (managers, coaches), need to change a performer's negative attitude to a positive one.
- Helps to focus & increase the likelihood of more consistent performances.

- Some attitudes are harder to change due to STEREOTYPES & wider social issues.

PERSUASIVE COMMUNICATION

- Persuasion through communication (verbal &/or physical) is effective, if delivered by a 'significant others' (influential person respected).
- The effectiveness depends on...
- If the 'persuader' is respected to a significant others.
- Appropriateness & quality of the message (makes sense, accurate & clear).
- The characteristics of the person being persuaded. Able to accept & understand the message.

STRATEGIES
(to change performers attitudes).

- Use positive role models to demonstrate positive attitudes.
- Give positive reinforcement of correct behaviour/attitudes.
- Agree targets/goals with the performer.
- Reward successful elements of performance.
- Give performers appropriate roles & responsibilities.

FESTINGER - COGNITIVE DISSONANCE THEORY (1957)

- States that all 3 elements involved with attitude (Triadic model - previous page) should be consistent if the attitude is to remain stable & create a feeling of CONSONANCE (positive attitude).

- If elements conflict (2 or more), this causes DISSONANCE (disharmony) leads to the person feeling uncomfortable & so attitudes are more likely to change due to the person wanting to become more comfortable, with ↑ belief dominant.

DRIVE THEORY

- Devised by HULL (1943) & then subsequently reviewed by SPENCE & SPENCE (1908).
- Drive Theory is ... a proportional linear relationship between arousal & performance. i.e. as arousal increases, performance increases in proportion to arousal.
- However, this is dependent on the learned DOMINANT RESPONSE
- For an elite athlete or a performer at the autonomous stage of learning, the DOMINANT RESPONSE tends to be correctly learnt & they are able to deal (appropriately) with higher levels of arousal.
- For a novice performer (beginner) in the cognitive stage of learning, the DOMINANT RESPONSE tends to be an incorrect action & there would be a decrease in performance. This would reflect a negative linear relationship between arousal & performance
- It is important to monitor the application of pressurised scenarios for novice performers as this may lead to a decrease in motivation - DRIVE REDUCTION

When looking at AROUSAL, various factors must be considered, including:

- situational factors
- stages of learning
- personality.
- task differences

AROUSAL

As well as Hull's DRIVE THEORY, the INVERTED U HYPOTHESIS & the CATASTROPHE THEORY must be covered (see pages 46-47).

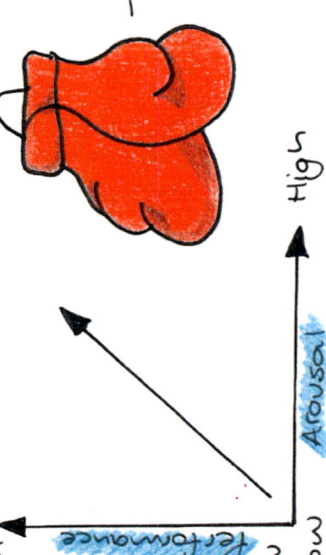

High | Performance — Low to High | Arousal

WEINBERG & GOULD (2007)

- Define arousal as .. 'a blend of physiological & psychological activity in a person and it refers to the level of motivation, alertness and excitement at a particular moment.'
- Arousal can also be defined (in short) as, 'the level of psychological readiness.'

EFFECTS OF AROUSAL

- The sports performer can be both OVER & UNDER aroused.
- Both of these can lead to a DECREASE in performance.
- This will affect a performer's concentration & motivation levels, both of which are closely linked to arousal levels.

INVERTED U HYPOTHESIS

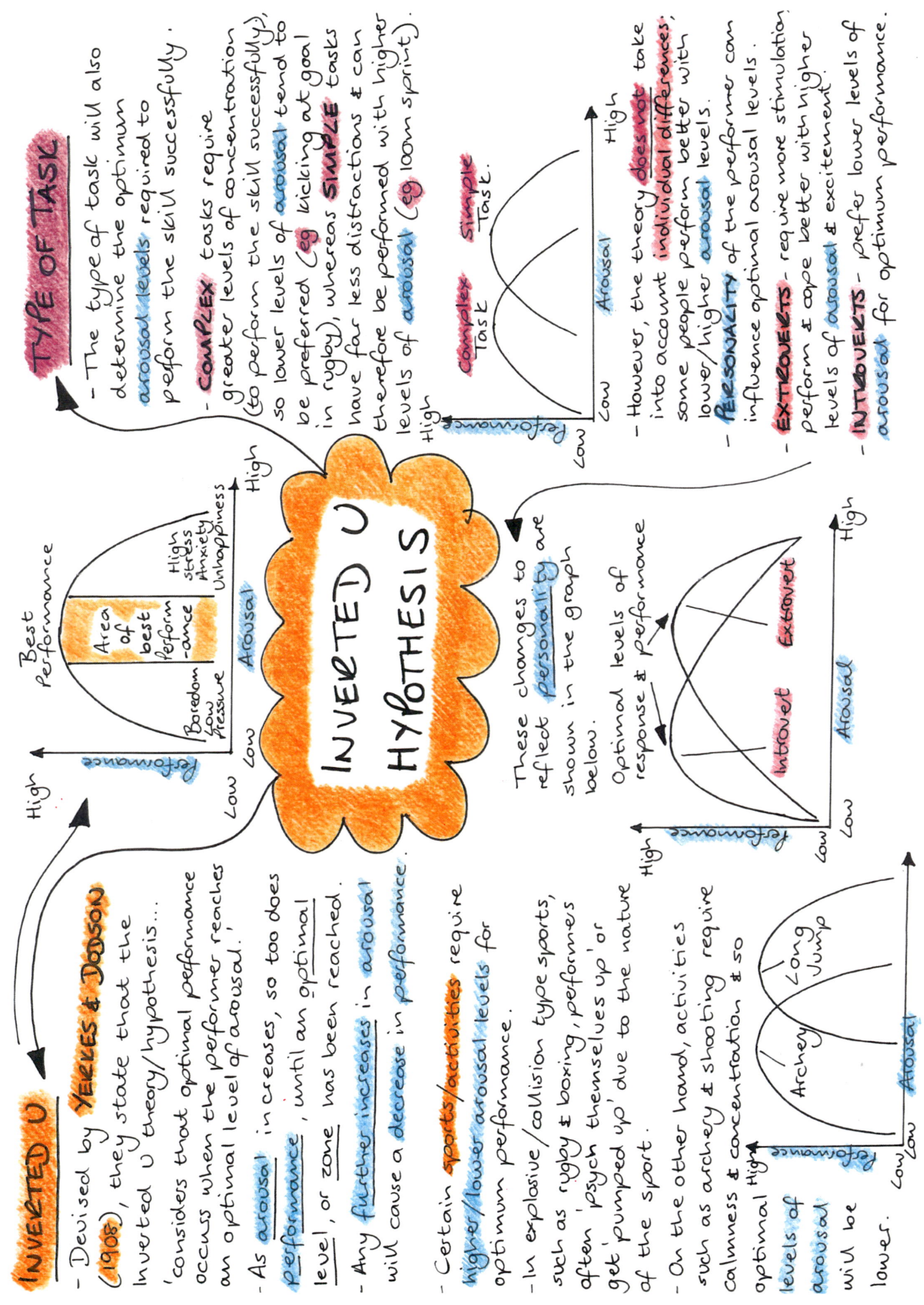

TYPE OF TASK

- The type of task will also determine the optimum arousal levels required to perform the skill successfully.

- **COMPLEX** tasks require greater levels of concentration (to perform the skill successfully), so lower levels of arousal tend to be preferred (eg kicking at goal in rugby), whereas **SIMPLE** tasks have far less distractions & can therefore be performed with higher levels of arousal (eg 100m sprint).

(graph: Performance vs Arousal, Low to High — Simple Task, Complex Task)

- However, the theory does not take into account individual differences; some people perform better with lower/higher arousal levels.

- **PERSONALITY** of the performer can influence optimal arousal levels.

- **EXTROVERTS** - require more stimulation, perform & cope better with higher levels of arousal & excitement.

- **INTROVERTS** - prefer lower levels of arousal for optimum performance.

INVERTED U

- Devised by **YERKES & DODSON** (1908), they state that the Inverted U theory/hypothesis... 'considers that optimal performance occurs when the performer reaches an optimal level of arousal.'

- As arousal increases, so too does performance, until an optimal level, or zone has been reached.

- Any further increases in arousal will cause a decrease in performance.

- Certain sports/activities require higher/lower arousal levels for optimum performance.

- In explosive/collision type sports, such as rugby & boxing, performers often 'psych themselves up' or get 'pumped up' due to the nature of the sport.

- On the other hand, activities such as archery & shooting require calmness & concentration & so optimal levels of arousal will be lower.

(graph: Performance vs Arousal — Boredom, Low pressure, Area of best performance, High stress, Anxiety, Unhappiness; Best Performance)

These changes to reflect personality are shown in the graph below. Optimal levels of response & performance.

(graph: Performance vs Arousal — Introvert, Extrovert)

(graph: Performance vs Arousal — Archery, Long Jump)

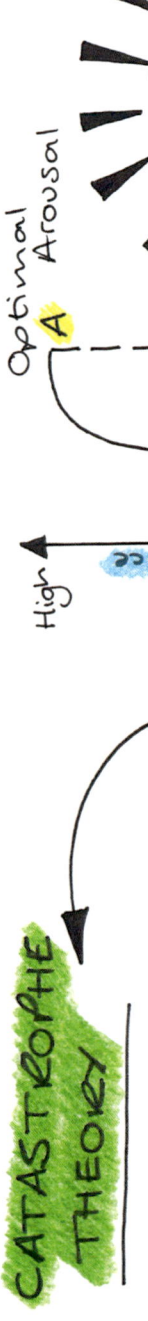

CATASTROPHE THEORY

- Increase in arousal outside of the performers comfort zone can increase their anxiety levels (state of nervousness).

- **HARDY & FAZEY (1988)** recognised that the catastrophe theory is a non-linear relationship between anxiety & performance.

- This theory recognises that continual mistakes made through a game/bout/event, lead to an increase in arousal, which in turn increases both...

- **SOMATIC** (physiological) and
- **COGNITIVE** (psychological) anxiety.

- As a result, this increase in anxiety (both types), leads to a **CATASTROPHIC** decline in performance.

CATASTROPHE THEORY

(centre)

- **COGNITIVE ANXIETY** (worry about performance) leads to high levels of
- **SOMATIC ANXIETY** (struggling to perform skills correctly).
- eg. A golfer plays a bad tee shot into the rough then continues to play bad shots subsequently, no matter what they do.

(Graph: Performance (vertical, Low to High) vs Arousal (horizontal, Low to High). Optimal Arousal marked at A, with points A, B, D, C)

POINT A
- Cognitive anxiety is high
- Somatic anxiety is low
- Result = performance is enhanced, hitting optimal levels.

POINT B
- Cognitive anxiety is high
- Somatic anxiety is high
- Result = performance levels can decline (very, very quickly).

POINT D
- Performance does not return to original level straight away (even though the performer tries to reduce arousal).

POINT C
- Performance levels continue to decrease/deteriorate.

TYPES OF ANXIETY

SPIELBERGER (1966) suggested that there are 2 different types of anxiety.

TRAIT ANXIETY

- Innate levels of anxiety that form part of 'our' personality.
- Performers with high trait anxiety have a tendency to be fearful of unfamiliar situations & perceive competitive scenarios as threatening. AKA ... Competitive trait anxiety (competition causes apprehension & tension).

STATE ANXIETY

- An emotional response to a particular situation - feel nervous & apprehensive.
- Often temporary & will depend on the performers interpretation of the stressfulness of the situation.
- Generally, people with high trait anxiety also have high state anxiety.
- eg Basketball - comfortable in the game, however will suffer from high state anxiety at the free throw line, especially late in the game if the score is close.

There are...

3 DIMENSIONS OF ANXIETY

- Cognitive
- Somatic
- Behavioural

& ...

2 TYPES OF ANXIETY

- Trait
- State

... to learn!

ANXIETY

LEVITT (1980) defines anxiety as ... ' the subjective feeling of apprehension and heightened psychological arousal often associated with fear, worries and doubts.'

THE THREE DIMENSIONS OF ANXIETY

SOMATIC

- Physiological response to a situation where the performer feels they may not cope.
- Tends to dissipate during a performance, therefore has minimal effect (for most performers).
- eg Increased heart rate, sweaty palms, muscle tension.

BEHAVIOURAL

- Feelings that lead to certain patterns of behaviour.
- Eg Biting fingernails, fidgeting, 'uncharacteristic behaviour' (can depend on their personality).

COGNITIVE

- Psychological response to a situation. Feelings of nervousness & apprehension.
- Irrational thinking & worries that may occur before & during a performance.
- 'Fear of failure'/believing they do not have the ability.
- It is these negative thoughts that have the biggest negative impact on performance.

THE EFFECTS OF ANXIETY ON PERFORMANCE

3 to consider...
- Zone of Optimal Functioning
- Catastrophe Theory
- Choking.

CATASTROPHE THEORY

Suggests...

- Stress & anxiety will influence performance.
- Each performer will respond in a unique way to competitive anxiety.
- Performance will be affected in an unique way & may be difficult to predict using general rules.
- As mentioned on page 47, this theory recognises that continual mistakes made throughout a game lead to an increase in arousal.
- This in turn increases both SOMATIC (physiological) & COGNITIVE (psychological) anxiety.
- The graph below shows the relation-ship between cognitive & somatic anxiety. Increases in cognitive anxiety have a negative linear relation-ship with performance, whereas somatic anxiety tends to mimic the Inverted U hypothesis.

SOMATIC / COGNITIVE — Performance vs Arousal (Low – High)

ZONE OF OPTIMAL FUNCTIONING

- Often referred to as... 'in the zone', 'state of flow', or 'peak flow experience', where performers feel they 'can do nothing wrong!'.
- When performers are in their optimal performance zone, this means they are experiencing their preferred level of anxiety & arousal.
- If a performer experiences too much or too little anxiety, this can hinder performance, as they are outside of their optimal zone.
- The 'zone of optimal functioning' is very individual & is experienced more regularly by expert/elite performers.

Maximum Performance — Zone of optimal functioning — Performance vs Arousal (Low – High)

CHOKING

- Refers to pervasive (common) problems in which there is a sudden impairment/failure of athletic performance due to anxiety.
- Characterised by cognitive anxiety & the feeling that 'the harder I try, the worse my performance.'
- Generally occurs on the 'big stage' or in 'big moments' when arousal levels are high (mainly cognitive), which can increase anxiety systems & stress & lead to a bad performance, especially when they should have won. Many, many egs including Newcastle 1996 'losing' the Premier League to Man. Utd.

COGNITIVE STRESS MANAGEMENT TECHNIQUES

MENTAL REHEARSAL / VISUALISATION

- Creating mental pictures of specific movements/actions executed in an actual game/event is a way of preparing for competition, reducing stress & making the performer feel more relaxed & prepared.

- Using mental pictures & specific sounds (of game/event) can create more realistic/vivid mental images.

IMAGERY

- Mental imagery can help with confidence & focus and at the same time, reduce anxiety.

- More experienced performers can use images of past performances (where they have been successful) to prepare, reinforcing their ability to perform well.

- Leads to an increase in confidence.

GOAL SETTING

- Setting clear goals can help a performer re-focus away from the source of stress & focus on more processes & performance goals.

- Setting realistic & achieveable goals can help to alleviate & reduce stress.

NEGATIVE THOUGHT STOPPING

- Performers can suffer from negative self talk, using phrases such as 'I am not going to win this', or 'my opponent is better than me'.

- Converting to more positive thinking & self talk will reduce negativity & provide more optimistic/focussed attitude.

POSITIVE THINKING / SELF TALK

- Using positive set phrases repeatedly can help reduce stress & anxiety, as the performer is able to focus the attention on performance instead of any negative thoughts they may have.

- Can also contribute to maintaining relevant arousal levels.

RATIONAL THINKING

- The way performers perceive certain situations is crucial to how they respond to certain stressors.

- In pressurised situations, performers can make (usual) decisions based on their perception eg: if they fear a situation due to the risk of injury, irrational decisions are likely to be made.

- Performers should be reassured during these situations.

- Training sessions planned to cater for a variety of scenarios to prepare for 'real-life' experiences.

- Should ensure more rational thinking on a regular basis.

MINDFULNESS

- Concentrating on 'the present' & it is quite often used in conjunction with meditation.

- Allows the performer to relax, reduce stress & anxiety & focus on the current task, not something in the future.

- eg a batter in cricket may be worried about getting into position for an insuing (bowl) rather than playing each ball on its merits.

Somatic Stress Management Techniques

Remember...
- **Cognitive** (psychological), focusses on the mind.
- **Somatic** (physiological), focusses on the body.

Pre-Game Routines
- Many coaches have a set routine for players/performers prior to the game.
- This may include some individual time, but the warm-up through to the game generally follows the same pattern. It is used in part to get players focussed & therefore reduce anxiety before a performance.
- Pre-game routines could be as simple as timings & type of food eaten, to superstitions.
  - eg underwear worn, or a 'ritual'
  - eg Pacific Island nations performing a Haka before a contest.

Biofeedback
- The use of physiological measuring equipment (i.e heart rate monitors, blood pressure data etc), so performers are aware of how their body responds to certain situations.
- Allows performers to understand their body more, to aid controlling their anxiety & stress levels.

Centering Technique
- Assists performers on how to focus on a strong point (the spot) in the body & to imagine being in that perfect state (the centre).
- Redirecting energy to the centre of the body through centring techniques such as imagery, use of cues & controlled breathing, maintaining a sense of calm.
- Aim - reduce anxiety and stress

Progressive Muscular Relaxation (PMR)
- The use of PMR is said to reduce muscle tension, improve sleep patterns & aid quicker overall recovery.
- It involves contraction & relaxation of muscles, usually working from one end of the body to the other.
- The contraction phase helps the performer feel the tension, whilst the relaxation phase assists in 'letting go' the tension.
- A hard technique to master & plenty of practice is required.

Breathing Control
- Reducing breathing rate by taking slow/longer breaths can not only assist in controlling heart rate, but reduce arousal levels & muscle tension.
- Deep inhalations allow for greater O$_2$ consumption & long controlled exhalations help dispense CO$_2$ as well as assisting the performer to focus on the task in hand.

AGGRESSION & ASSERTION

TYPES OF AGGRESSION
- Hostile
- CHANNELLED
- REACTIVE
- INSTRUMENTAL

AGGRESSION
- Is a term that is used in different ways, though it is important to distinguish between desirable and undesirable behaviours.
- BARON (1977) defines aggression as... 'any behaviour directed at the goal of harming or injuring another being who is motivated to avoid such treatment.'
  - eg punching someone in rugby.

ASSERTION...
On the other hand is generally defined as...'forceful behaviour that is controlled and within the laws of the game.'
- eg a perfectly timed tackle in rugby when contact is made around the waist & the tackler wins the collision.

CHANNELLED
- No intention to harm & within the rules & spirit of the game.
- Looking to play/compete with authority.
  - eg playing strong and powerful shots in tennis to score points quickly & finish off rallies on their own terms.

INSTRUMENTAL
- Aggressive behaviours that is inside the rules of the game, however is used to either cause harm, exploit weakness or intimidate.
- eg a cricket team may use a fast bowler to bowl short deliveries directed at the head/body to either intimidate or get them to play a bad shot (or set them up for another tactic).

REACTIVE
- Similar to hostile aggression, this also refers to aggressive behaviours that occur outside the rules of the game & with the intent to harm, but it is a reaction/retaliation to other aggressive acts.
- eg a high tackle in rugby results in a team mate hitting the opponent/instigator.

HOSTILE
- Refers to aggressive behaviours that occur outside the rules of the game & the intent to harm.
- eg a two footed tackle in football.

52

THEORIES OF AGGRESSION

FRUSTRATION – AGGRESSION HYPOTHESIS

- **DOLLARD** (1939) suggested that when a goal is blocked, frustration can occur, which in turn leads to aggressive behaviours.

- Closely linked to the instinct theory, once aggressive behaviours have been implemented, levels of frustration decrease, leading to catharsis (emotional release)

- This is only true if the act of aggression leads to success.

- If it is unsuccessful, more frustration can occur.

Catharsis ← Success

Drive → Obstacle → Frustration → Aggression
          to goal

Punishment

SOCIAL LEARNING THEORY

- **BANDURA** (1971) believed that aggression is based on modelling/observing, which can in turn lead to behaviours being mimicked due to their experiences.

- This is why leaders & coaches have a duty to ensure rules are adhered to & any aggressive behaviours outside of the rules of the game are dealt with some type of consequence.

INSTINCT THEORY

- Proposed by **FREUD** (1933), but researched further by **LORENZ** et al (1966).

- Suggests that aggression is genetically inherited & that we are biologically determined to act aggressively in an attempt to become dominant (though everyone has their own levels of innate aggression).

- **LORENZ** believed that aggressive energy can build up & needs to be released; sport can provide a 'perfect platform' for acceptable aggressive behaviour to be released.

AGGRESSIVE CUE HYPOTHESIS

- **BERKOWITZ** (1969) believed that frustration leads to an increase in arousal, but not immediate aggression.

- This depends on the situation & whether or not there are aggressive cues.

- if the sport lends itself to more aggressive acts (such as a collision sport like rugby league), then there is a greater chance of aggressive behaviour if frustration develops.

Frustration
eg blocking of a goal → Increased arousal
eg anger → Presence of aggressive → greater likelihood of aggression
no aggressive cues → less likelihood of aggression

53

STRATEGIES TO REDUCE AGGRESSION

- **Punishments.** This type of behaviour has consequences; fines, suspensions, loss of position on the team.

- **Encourage non-aggressive** role models.

- **Change position**, remove the aggressive player from the situation. eg substitute off.

- **Implement stress management** cognitive/relaxation techniques.

- Use **positive reinforcement** for non-aggressive behaviour & **negative reinforcement** for aggressive behaviour.

- Look to **change/modify** the performers perception. eg 'reframe' the situation.

- **Rewards** given out now to highlight fair play. eg the FIFA Fair Play Award.

- Aggression/Assertion
- Theories of Aggression
- Types of Aggression
- Causes of Aggression
- Strategies to reduce Aggression.

AGGRESSION

- **Bracketed morality.** A temporary suspension during competition of the high level of ethical morality necessary for everyday life.
  - i.e do not consider the needs/desires of anyone else due to the different environment the performer is in (on the pitch). Some performers may see the sporting arena as a 'different environment' to everyday life, so morals are different. eg politeness is not required, especially to the opposition, so sledging is ok!

CAUSES OF AGGRESSION

- **Nature of the game** (collision or contact) eg rugby league.

- **Hostile crowds** that increase arousal levels leading to aggressive behaviour. eg derby match in football.

- **Frustration.** Could be caused by poor performance, goals blocked, refereeing decisions, opposition baiting/sledging.

- **Rivalry** eg The Ashes in cricket, Man Utd v Liverpool.

- **Reaction** to dirty play, provocation by opponent. eg Zidane in World Cup final 2006.

- **Under developed moral reasoning.** The maturity of an athlete's moral reasoning can determine levels of aggressive behaviour. Some research suggests that some performers with lower moral reasoning are more likely to act aggressively & injure their opponent in their pursuit of success/goal.

- 'Win at all costs' attitude.
... why not?

TYPES OF MOTIVATION

(central node: TYPES OF MOTIVATION)

MAEHR & ZUSHO (2009) define
motivation as... 'the process that influences the initiation, direction, magnitude or intensity, perseverance, continuation and quality of a goal-directed behaviour.'

IN SHORT... 'motivation
has two aspects: it is what drives us to do things... and makes us do particular things.' WOODS (1998)

Motivation has 2 main dimensions; intensity & direction.

INTENSITY - is concerned with arousal, which determines the amount of effort that is given to achieving a set of goals... DIRECTION.

NEGATIVE MOTIVATION

- This response is characterised by an improvement in performance out of a fear of not performing well.
- Although some type of negative motivation techniques may be needed in small doses (at elite level), some coaches use this too much & unfortunately negative motivation may decrease an athletes self-esteem & self-confidence.
- eg a player may train really hard, not for the sole reason of improving performance or fitness, but to reduce the chance of being yelled at or ridiculed by the coach!

INTRINSIC MOTIVATION

- The internal drive to succeed, where performers possess their own personal ambition, to have fun & enjoyment
- A sense of pride by achieving a goal are also factors for high intrinsic levels of motivation (intangible rewards such as recognition & sense of achievement).
- Making training fun & enjoyable aswell as balancing the competitive aspect is key to success in sport
- Longevity usually based on higher levels of intrinsic motivation & closely linked to arousal levels. If a performer does not get the same enjoyment or sense of achievement as previously, arousal levels will not be in the optimum zone & so intrinsic motivation decreases.

POSITIVE MOTIVATION

- Is a response that takes place when an individuals performance is driven by previous reinforcing behaviours.
- Relies on continual self reinforcement by external sources (such as coach, family, peers, spectators & the media).
- Positive motivation techniques can be used to enhance this response. eg clear communication, continual praise & encouragement.

EXTRINSIC MOTIVATION

- Extrinsic factors that drive a performer to succeed, or tangible rewards, such as money, trophies, big contracts as well as fame & pressure from other people.
- In the early or cognitive stage of learning, reinforcement through rewards & praise can be used to strengthen extrinsic motivation.
- However, this must be balanced carefully with intrinsic motivation as the performer progresses through the stages of learning.
- eg a Tour de France cyclist may be motivated to win the race & the fame that comes with it (extrinsic motivation & extrinsic reward) but can also gain satisfaction & enjoyment from the task (intrinsic motivation & intrinsic reward).

55

NACH - NEED TO ACHIEVE

- The people have 'approach behaviours' & tend to seek challenging situations.

- The performers are <u>not</u> afraid of failure & seek criticism in order to improve performance.

- They set high goals & take risks in the pursuit of success or improvement in standard.

- However, there is a high value to success.

- A boxer with a NACH personality type may approach this challenge as they <u>do not</u> fear failure & are <u>motivated</u> to succeed.

- On the flip side for the heavy -weight champion, there is a high probability of success, but little value & satisfaction to be gained from winning, as it is <u>expected</u>.

- Therefore there will be <u>little</u> motivation to take on this bout, especially if they are more <u>intrinsically motivated</u> as an extrovert.

THEORIES OF MOTIVATION

FACTORS THAT INFLUENCE BEHAVIOUR

- SITUATIONAL FACTORS - affect motivation for performance, generally influenced by the probability of success or failure & the rewards that can be gained as a result.

- eg. if there is a <u>difficult task</u> (beating the heavyweight champion in boxing), there is a low probability of success for a new heavyweight boxer.

ACHIEVEMENT MOTIVATION

- ATKINSON & McCLELLAND (1953) both proposed that achievement motivation comes from the individual's personality. It is their motivation to strive for success.

- The concept links personality to competitiveness.

ACHIEVEMENT MOTIVATION

ACHIEVEMENT = INTRINSIC MOTIVATION

COGNITIVE STATE ANXIETY

Achievement motivation has 2 dimensions...

NAF - Need to Avoid Failure

NACH - Need to Achieve

NAF - NEED TO AVOID FAILURE

- These people have 'avoidance behaviours' & are intent on avoiding competitive situations.

- Performers with NAF personalities/ personality types have lowered to achieve, fear failure & lack a competitive edge (this could be due to learned helplessness).

- Performers will generally select low goals (as this will give them some kind of achievement) or very high goals (as the expectation of them succeeding is low).

- However, praise may be awarded for attempting such a situation (chronic failure syndrome).

GOAL SETTING & MOTIVATION

There are 4 main types of goals to learn for developing & enhancing motivation.
- Mastery
- Outcome
- Socially approved
- Task orientated

OUTCOME GOALS

- ... sometimes called

EGO GOALS.
- Motivated by winning.
- These type of goals are only recommended for the 'elite-performer' in top level competitions, & not for performers in the early/ cognitive stage of learning.

SOCIALLY APPROVED GOALS

- These goals are set to improve on weaknesses in performance.
- Seek to get external approval & reinforcement to help increase motivation.
- eg receiving positive reinforcement from a captain or coach that you have performed your role in a 'set play/move' correctly.

TASK ORIENTATED GOALS

- Desire to win.
- ... however the process is about perfecting certain tasks within a performance as a way of improving performance overall (in the long run).
- eg improving 1st serve success rate in tennis will lead to greater performance overall.

MASTERY GOALS

- ... or PROCESS GOALS.
- Can be used to help set targets for improvement in a performance.
- These goals are not necessarily focussed on the overall result.
- They are more about achieving & mastering goals that are broken down in order to eventually achieve an overall goal.
- Generally associated with mastering a technical element.
- eg (improving a certain aspect of performance) such as the technical efficiency of a somersault within a trampolining routine.

GOAL SETTING

- There is more about goal setting later in the book (page 62-3), focussed on the SMARTER principle & their use, importance & effectiveness in optimising performance.

The effect of Social Facilitation

Performance (y-axis: High / Low) vs Arousal (x-axis: Low / High)

SOCIAL FACILITATION

- Refers to how the presence of an audience/crowd positively enhances performance.

As arousal increases, there is a greater likelihood of the DOMINANT RESPONSE occurring. In the case of an elite performer, the dominant response is more than likely to be the correct one, improving performance (SOCIAL FACILITATION).

SOCIAL INHIBITION

- Refers to the negative effect on performance due to the attendance of an audience/crowd.

- ZAJONC (1965) found that the mere presence of others is sufficient to increase the arousal levels of a performer linking closely with the DRIVE THEORY (p45). He grouped the 'others' into 2 categories...

  PASSIVE
  INTERACTIVE

HOWEVER

- For a performer in the early/cognitive stage of learning, the DOMINANT RESPONSE is likely to be incorrect.
- This will therefore have an adverse & detrimental effect on performance (SOCIAL INHIBITION). It may reflect a negative line & some of the information with regards the INVERTED U HYPOTHESIS (see page 46) will/may apply.

- The same concept applies to fine & complex skills being performed in the presence of others.
- The increased levels of arousal will increase the likelihood of an incorrect execution.
- ...whereas the performance of simple & gross skills will increase the likelihood of a correct response & positive execution.

PASSIVE

- Audience & co-actors.
- Does not have a big influence on performance compared to interactive others...
- Unless the performer feels that one of the passive others is 'significant' to them & they have the feeling they may be assessed.
- Leads to higher anxiety levels.

INTERACTIVE

- Competitors & spectators.
- Has a greater impact on performance.
- Competitors can directly influence a performance physically & spectators can increase arousal levels.
- This is especially true if the crowd is close to play (proximity effect) & playing away from home.

58

SOCIAL FACILITATION & INHIBITION

EVALUATION APPREHENSION

- COTTRELL (1968) suggested that it is <u>not</u> the presence of others that leads to an increase in arousal, it is whether or not the performer <u>perceives</u> that the audience/crowd is assessing or judging their performance.
- However, if there were scouts present evaluating her performance, then her arousal levels & anxiety levels could increase... as a result of EVALUATION APPREHENSION.
- eg a young netballer may be calm with an audience watching her play.

STRATEGIES TO MINIMISE SOCIAL INHIBITION

- Practice selective attention.
- Use imagery &/or mental rehearsal to block out the audience/crowd.
- Ensure skills over-learnt.
- Introduce evaluative others into practice - allows performer to get used to the process.
- Appropriate use of attribution.
- Stress management techniques in training.
- Greater awareness of appropriate arousal levels & zone of optimal functioning.

Presence of others → Arousal → Dominant Response

If Dominant Response is incorrect → Process loss

If Dominant Response is correct → Process gain

EFFECTS ON PERFORMANCE of Social Facilitation

- It is no surprise that most teams playing at home have a higher win percentage than those playing away.
- This can mainly be attributed to familiar surroundings & a more supportive home crowd.
- However, this could work against the home team if they are on a 'losing streak', or in tight situations (close result), that could ultimately lead to 'choking'. (see page 49).

- The PROXIMITY EFFECT can also affect arousal & anxiety levels. Sports such as basketball & netball have crowds that are very close to the action, creating a more hostile environment for the away team.
- ... whereas some football & rugby stadia (mainly newer grounds) set crowds back from the action
- The recent Corona-virus pandemic has negated this home advantage with games being played for large chunks of time behind closed doors.

GROUP & TEAM DYNAMICS

CARRON's FOUR FACTORS OF GROUP COHESION

ENVIRONMENTAL FACTORS.
- Factors that help bind groups together include age, location, employment & ethos.
- Holding camps, equal importance & value amongst the group can improve group cohesion.

PERSONAL FACTORS.
- Refers to the belief in the group, a desire to win & social relationships within community/group.
- Desire to achieve excellence generally shared & it is important in avoiding the formation of cliques.

LEADERSHIP FACTORS.
- The influence of the coach or manager is important in building identity.
- Leaders can improve cohesion by affiliation through task & social cohesion factors (eg Sir Alex Ferguson, Pep Guardiola).

TEAM FACTORS.
- The team or group should have a clear identity, with set targets & every member of that group feeling that they have a role in the team.

There are 2 theories to consider with regard to group / team dynamics. These are...
- Carron
- Steiner
- Plus Ringlemann effect.

A GROUP
- SHAW (1976) defines a group as... 'two or more people interacting with one another in a manner that each person influences and is influenced by each other person.

GROUP DYNAMICS
- Refers to ... 'the processes operating within the group between individual members.

- CARRON (1980) stated that a cohesive group will have the following characteristics...
  - a collective identity
  - a sense of shared purpose
  - structured patterns of communication

TASK COHESION
- The way team members work together to successfully complete a task.
- eg all working together to complete a set penalty corner tactic in hockey successfully.

SOCIAL COHESION
- The interaction & relationship within a group.
- eg having a strong bond during the Olympic period or on a cricket tour will improve group cohesion.

60

STEINER & RINGLEMANN EFFECT

STRATEGIES TO DEVELOP GROUP COHESION

- Holding training camps to build unity.
- Ensure all members of the group have equal value & importance.
- rewarding all players equally with praise/criticism.
- mixing young/old together (players), or different subgroups.
- developing a shared responsibility for success.
- avoiding the formation of cliques.
- identifying why members individually want to be part of the group (building their motives).
- identifying those who exhibit 'social loafing' & introduce methods to incorporate them into the group.
- unite players in their belief of the leader, through leadership style & behaviour (mix of autocratic/democratic - more later on page 70), that is
- incorporate a 'leadership group' that is approachable for players.
- avoid criticising individuals in front of the group.
- get to know the team. Be aware of each players needs & their preferred way of interacting & style of motivation.
- Appropriate use of team goals in the short, medium & big term.
- clear member roles in the group as integral to the team ethic (avoid Ringlemann effect).

Losses Due To Faulty Processes (FP)
= Factors that can go wrong in team performance which impede/prevent group cohesion.

Potential Productivity (PP)
= The maximum capability of the group when cohesiveness is strongest.

Actual Productivity (AP)
= The team performance at any given time (due to successful interaction).

STEINER
- Group cohesion is the force that binds a group together, helping prevent faulty processes (i.e. losses due to poor form, reduced motivation & lack of teamwork).
- A team full of great individuals is not always the best formula, especially if there are faulty processes that lead to a lack of cohesion.
- for STEINER (1972), in order for a group to perform to their potential, essential team strategies need to be implemented that motivate & improve group productivity & also reduce the chance of SOCIAL motivation loss due to SOCIAL LOAFING.

RINGLEMANN EFFECT & SOCIAL LOAFING
According to RINGLEMANN (1974) when working in groups, an individuals performance will decrease. Why?
- Co-ordination losses where 'operational effectiveness' of the group cannot be sustained for the whole match. eg lineout execution wrong due to bad timing of jump & positional issues.
- Co-ordination problems more likely as size of group increases.

- Motivation losses can also lead to lack of effort, especially in a big group (not everyone has a defined role).
- Individuals may think others will 'pick up the slack' - this is known as SOCIAL LOAFING.
- devise & identify a clear system of rewards & punishments - group help devise.
- encourage social bonding through social events.

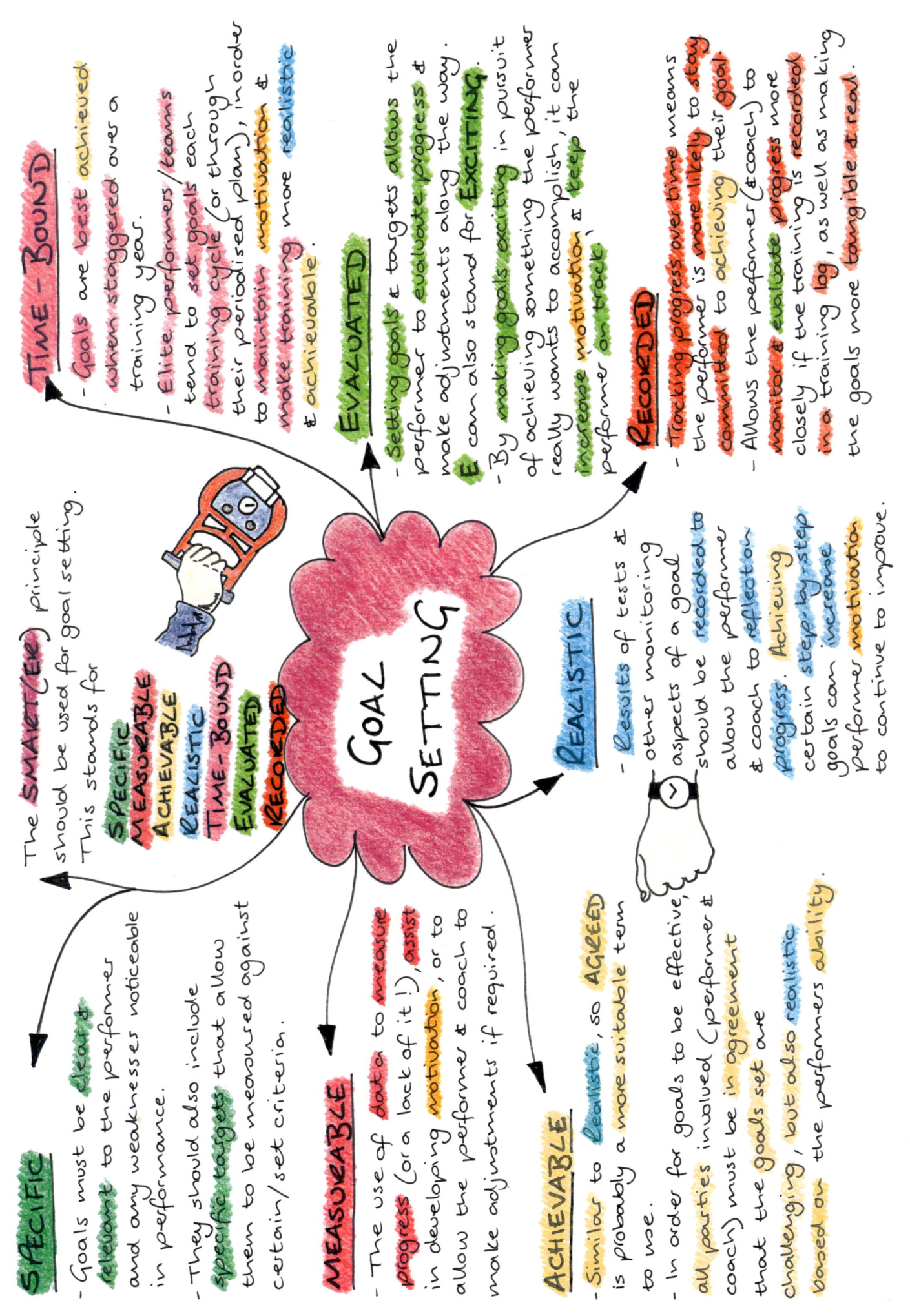

GOAL SETTING

The SMART(ER) principle should be used for goal setting. This stands for
Specific
Measureable
Achievable
Realistic
Time-Bound
Evaluated
Recorded

TIME-BOUND
- Goals are best achieved when staggered over a training year.
- Elite performers/teams tend to set goals each training cycle (or through their periodised plan), in order to maintain motivation & make training more realistic & achievable.

EVALUATED
- Setting goals & targets allows the performer to evaluate progress & make adjustments along the way. E can also stand for EXCITING.
- By making goals exciting in pursuit of achieving something the performer really wants to accomplish, it can increase motivation & keep the performer on track.

RECORDED
- Tracking progress over time means the performer is more likely to stay committed to achieving their goal.
- Allows the performer (& coach) to monitor & evaluate progress more closely if the training is recorded in a training log, as well as making the goals more tangible & real.

REALISTIC
- Results of tests & others monitoring aspects of a goal should be recorded to allow the performer & coach to reflection progress. Achieving certain step-by-step goals can increase performer motivation to continue to improve.

SPECIFIC
- Goals must be clear & relevant to the performer and any weaknesses noticeable in performance.
- They should also include specific targets that allow them to be measured against certain/set criteria.

MEASUREABLE
- The use of data to measure progress (or a lack of it!), assist in developing motivation, or to allow the performer & coach to make adjustments if required.

ACHIEVABLE
- Similar to Realistic, so AGREED is probably a more suitable term to use.
- In order for goals to be effective, all parties involved (performer & coach) must be in agreement that the goals set are challenging, but also realistic based on the performer's ability.

GOAL SETTING

SHORT-TERM
- In order to achieve a LONG-term goal, a series of short term goals should be set, or goals that have been periodised.
- eg a netballer will periodise her training & have a separate focus for each phase of training to achieve peak fitness at certain times.

MEDIUM-TERM
- Goals set at certain points to encourage & maintain motivation. Particularly important for Olympic athletes or for sports with a long season.
- eg an Olympic athlete may have a medium term goal of winning a national competition before setting their sights on the long term goal of Olympic Gold!

LONG-TERM
- Ultimate goals to achieve at the end of a training programme or what you are in pursuit of.
- eg to be a kg after a 16 week training programme or to win Gold at the next Olympic Games.

TYPES OF GOALS TO OPTIMISE PERFORMANCE
Goals can be...
- SUBJECTIVE
- OBJECTIVE
- OUTCOME
- PERFORMANCE
- PROCESS
- REALISTIC & ASPIRATIONAL

& set in the SHORT, MEDIUM & LONG-TERM.

IMPORTANCE & EFFECTIVENESS
of goal setting. Why set them?

FOR ATTENTIONAL FOCUS
- Allows performers to focus on the important factors & cues in order to improve performance.

PERSISTENCE ON TASKS
- Setting goals can motivate performers to continue in their 'pursuit of perfection' of a certain skill, task or to improve an area of weakness.

RAISING CONFIDENCE & SELF EFFICACY
- Setting performance (improving end performance) & process (usually part of a performance/skill) goals can allow a performer to gradually gain confidence in certain situations.
- This will eventually lead to a better overall level of performance.

CONTROL OF AROUSAL & ANXIETY
- Setting goals will not only assist in improving confidence & motivation but it will increase the chances of controlling arousal & anxiety (optimal arousal zone).

MONITOR PERFORMANCE
- Goals can be broken down into short, medium & long term.
- Progress can be measured through a training programme.
- This will in turn increase motivation & lead to greater progress being made.

TYPES OF GOALS

OUTCOME / PRODUCT
- Also known as goals.
- Focus on achieving success in a competitive situation (game, tournament, competition).
- The target (goal) is based on the end result & is concerned with the outcome of the competition.

PERFORMANCE
- Goals that focus on achieving performance based on previous performances, not in comparison to others.
- Provide 'stepping stones' to improve the overall outcome.
- Enhance motivation & confidence.
- eg improving an overhead clear in badminton in order to force the opponent to the back of the court, to establish a better position to play more attacking shots.

PROCESS
- Focus on specific actions that need to be achieved during a performance & are mainly focussed on a specific skill / technique
- eg improving tumble turns in swimming in order to improve the overall outcome goal of winning the race.

SUBJECTIVE
- Are goals based on opinions & feelings.
- Are they general & generic?
- Goals should be specific with clear targets.
- ... however, activities such as dance & gymnastics may have more subjective goals, based on the subjective nature of how the quality of performance is assessed.

OBJECTIVE
- These goals can be measured with quantifiable data.
- eg training logs, notational data, video analysis, fitness tests.
- These types of goals make it much easier to track & monitor progress made by the performer.

REALISTIC & ASPIRATIONAL
- Goals should be realistic (in that they can be achieved) ... however they must also be aspirational & challenging to motivate & inspire a performer to train hard to accomplish the overall goal.
- The performer therefore will be more likely to maintain motivation & continue with their training.

WEINER'S MODEL OF ATTRIBUTION

- WEINER (1974) identified
  - Ability
  - Effort
  - Task Difficulty
  - Luck
- ... as the most important factors affecting achievement
- It has **3½** main dimensions...
  - Causality
  - Stability
  - Controllability

LOCUS OF CAUSALITY

- This dimension is mainly linked to whether the attributions are **internal** (with performers) or **external** eg environmental.
  - Ability & effort are seen as internal factors.
  - Task difficulty & luck are seen as external factors (outside the control of the performers).

Causality
Internal | External

| Ability | Task Difficulty |
| Effort | Luck |

Stability: stable / unstable

WEINER'S ATTRIBUTION THEORY

STABILITY

- Is referring to whether the reasons/causes were relatively permanent (stable) or changeable (unstable) in relation to time.
  - Ability & task difficulty are seen as being stable factors (in relation to time).
  - Effort & luck are changeable, therefore seen as unstable.

ATTRIBUTION THEORY

- Seeks to explain how individuals & teams elevate their levels of success & failure.
- It also seeks to show how the reasons given by an individual or team, or how they perceive their success or failure, may affect future **motivation** in similar situations.

CONTROLLABILITY

- Helps to explain the effective consequences of attributions that appear to be in a person's control (or not).
- This dimension has been shown to relate to the intensity of a performers personal feeling of satisfaction & pride, shame & guilt.
- **Motivation**, pride etc will increase if a performer relates their success to internal causes (eg ability & effort), rather than external uncontrollable factors.
- The opposite effect will generally occur if failure is also attributed to internal & controllable factors.
- Shame, dissatisfaction & loss of **motivation** are likely.

WEINER'S ADAPTED PROCESS OF ATTRIBUTION

The Difference Between High & Low Achievers

- HIGH achievers would attribute success to internal factors & attribute failure to unstable factors, therefore more motivated in achievement success.

- Low achievers tend to attribute success to external factors (eg luck) with failure attributed to stable factors, therefore find achievement situations less satisfying/less motivated.

- A performer's attribution will also be affected by whether they view success in terms of outcome goals or mastery goals.

- Performers who are more mastery orientated and not concerned with their performance (in comparison to others) focus on the ability to learn & master new skills in order to develop a fuller understanding of the task/sport.

- eg a netball shooter judging performance on previous set targets (mastery goals) - increase shot success rate if they will have greater feelings of pride than the centre who's focussed on outcome goals.

- Performers applying the attribution theory tend to show a SELF SERVING BIAS.

- i.e. a good performance is usually attributed to external & unstable factors (eg luck - 'a lucky shot'), or a poor performance is usually attributed to internal & stable factors.

The model or process for this can be seen below...

EVENT OUTCOME

AVAILABLE INFORMATION ON EVENT (previous record - own & opponents' win/loss record, referee, crowd, mood etc).

CAUSAL ATTRIBUTION internal/external, intentional/unintentional, stable/unstable.

EXPECTANCY (anticipation of future wins/losses)

AFFECTIVE RESPONSE (feelings of pride & shame).

DECISION FOR SUBSEQUENT PARTICIPATION (persistence with involvement in sport).

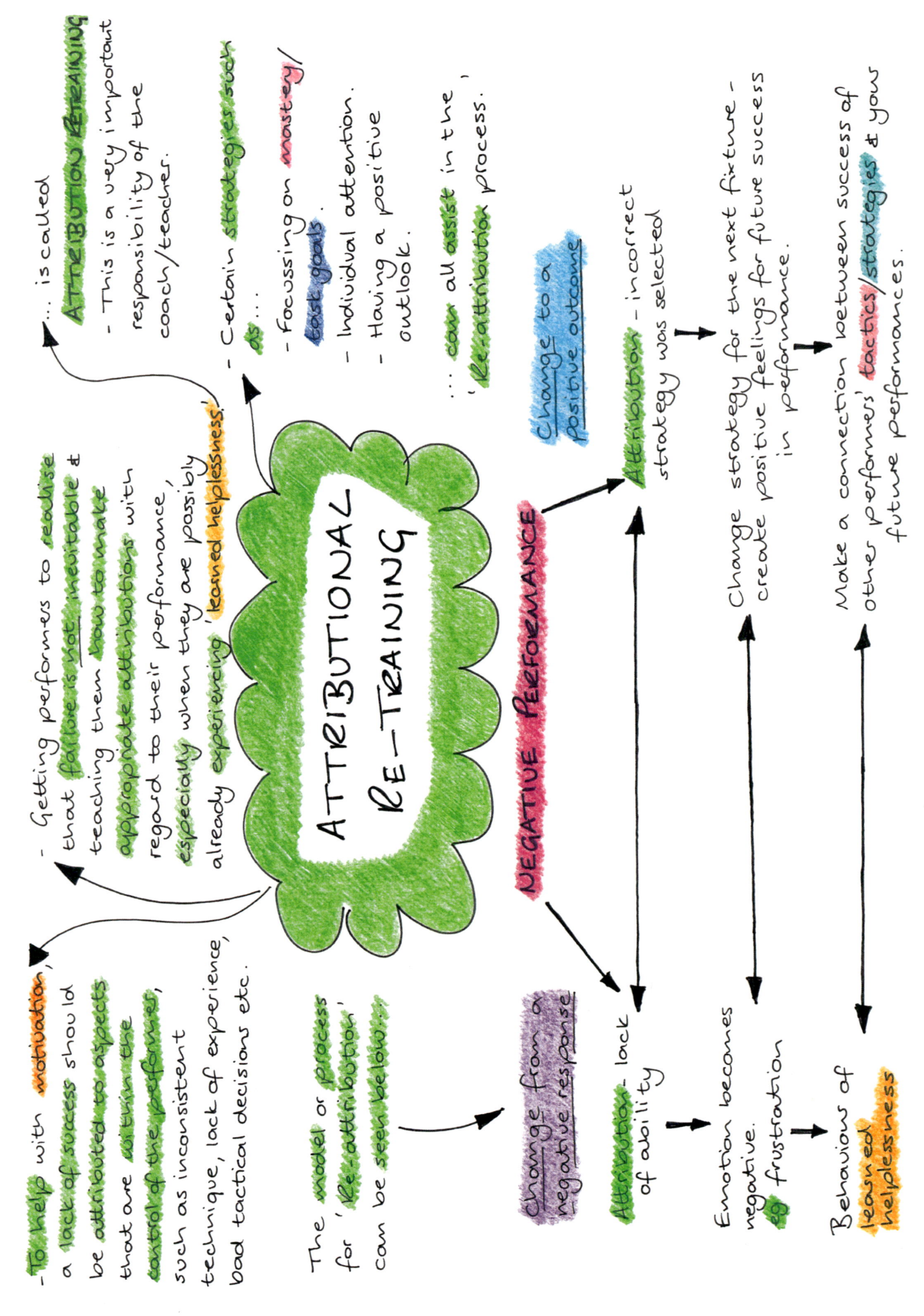

...is called

ATTRIBUTION RE-TRAINING

– This is a very important responsibility of the coach/teacher.

– Certain strategies such as...
– Focussing on mastery/task goals.
– Individual attention.
– Having a positive outlook.
...can all assist in the 're-attribution process.'

– Getting performers to realise that failure is not inevitable & teaching them how to make appropriate attributions with regard to their performance, especially when they are possibly already experiencing 'learned helplessness.'

– To help with motivation, a lack of success should be attributed to aspects that are within the control of the performer, such as inconsistent technique, lack of experience, bad tactical decisions etc.

The model or process for 're-attribution' can be seen below.

ATTRIBUTIONAL RE-TRAINING

NEGATIVE PERFORMANCE

Change from a negative response → Attribution - lack of ability → Emotion becomes negative. eg frustration → Behaviour of learned helplessness

Change to a positive outcome → Attribution - incorrect strategy was selected → Change strategy for the next fixture - create positive feelings for future success in performance. → Make a connection between success of other performers' tactics/strategies & your future performances.

VEALEY'S MODEL OF SPORT-SPECIFIC CONFIDENCE

VEALEY'S MODEL

- VEALEY (1986) proposed a sport specific theory of confidence and defined sport confidence as...

'the belief or degree of certainty individuals possess about their ability to be successful in sport.'

SELF-CONFIDENCE

- ... is defined as ... 'the sureness or degree of certainty of feeling that you are equal to the task or challenge.'

A sporting example (basketball free throw) will be used to outline Vealey's model.

THE SPORT SITUATION

- Shooting a free throw

TRAIT SPORTS CONFIDENCE

- This is the (innate) level of confidence (natural) possessed & is relatively stable.

- Relates to general ability to succeed in all sporting activities.

COMPETITIVE ORIENTATION

- Extent to which the performer is prepared to compete to succeed.

- 'Do you want to get the shot in because you want to win or just add to your statistics?'

STATE SPORTS CONFIDENCE

- Can be developed through learning & is unstable

- Relates to the belief about ability to succeed in a particular sport or situation in a sport. eg confidence in shooting a free throw.

- influenced by trait sports confidence & performers competitive orientation

PERFORMANCE

- Execution of the free throw.

SUBJECTIVE OUTCOME

- Perception of the outcome of the skill through feedback (internal & external).

- If the performer perceives the outcome was successful, this will increase trait sports confidence, competitiveness & state sports confidence. The opposite will occur if the outcome is perceived as negative.

IMPACT OF SPORTS CONFIDENCE

PERFORMANCE

- Having high levels of sports confidence will generally lead to greater motivation to achieve success (both within training and competition/games).

PARTICIPATION

- High levels of self confidence enables the individual to be able to integrate more with team activities & not feel apprehensive in their ability to contribute.

SELF-ESTEEM

- Performers with high levels of self confidence will often have high levels of self esteem. This helps to reduce anxiety levels for optimal arousal that can potentially improve performance.

Competitive Orientation

The Sport Situation eg free throw

Trait Sport Confidence

State Sports Confidence

Performance

Subjective Outcome

PERFORMANCE ACCOMPLISHMENTS

- High levels of previous success will lead to high self efficacy (& vice versa).

- Coaches & teachers must balance their sessions as some learners/ performers may not have experienced any success before so differentiated goals may need to be set.

VICARIOUS EXPERIENCES

- Watching others, especially of a similar ability succeed in sport will give the observer higher self efficacy & the feeling they can succeed.

- eg if a student is reluctant to join a basketball club, but observes a friend performing well in a session, he/she is more likely to join in.

VERBAL PERSUASION

- A message from a significant other, ie a respected leader is more likely to increase self efficacy as long as the message is believable & inspiring.

- If not, then the message is ignored & there is no (positive) effect on self confidence.

SELF EFFICACY

- ... is defined as 'the level of self confidence in any given situation or situational specific self confidence.'

- BANDURA (1977) identified 4 key factors in the development of self efficacy & the expectation of future success.

```
Performance Accomplishments ─┐
                             ├─→ Efficacy
Vicarious Experiences ───────┤    Expectations ─→ Athletic Performance
                             │
Verbal Persuasion ───────────┤
                             │
Emotional Arousal ───────────┘
```

SELF EFFICACY

LEARNED HELPLESSNESS

It is an acquired state related to the performers perception that they have no control over the situation, with failure/defeat being inevitable. Characteristics include...

- specific to one activity or general (global) to all activities.
- performer usually outcome orientated.
- from previous bad experiences.
- perceptions of low ability.
- rarely tries new skills.
- initial failure of new skills confirms perceptions.
- feelings of embarrassment.
- future effort limited.
- lacks motivation.
- feels incompetent.

EMOTIONAL AROUSAL

- If the performer feels under-aroused, then they will lack confidence.

- Being in the optimum arousal zone will increase confidence.

- This will ultimately lead to an improvement in performance.

69

LEADERSHIP STYLES

3 to consider...

AUTOCRATIC

- Take control & dictate the rules & expectations.
- Seen more when teaching novice athletes & when a decision is needed quickly in a dangerous situation or game saving scenario.
- Not recommended for elite performers as creativity & freedom of expression (of their talents) will be hampered.

DEMOCRATIC

- 'Person related' leadership style.
- Strong inter-personal skills.
- Leader listens to opinions of the group & shares the decision making process.
- Leader still has/makes the final decision when required.
- Most leaders apply all styles, though a more democratic approach has been the most consistent.

Leaders can be a combination of **EMERGENT & PRESCRIBED**; eg team captain selected by the coach & also voted in by the players.

CHARACTERISTICS OF EFFECTIVE LEADERS

There is NO single quality or clear guidelines on what the specific qualities of an effective leader are.

- ...however the factors listed below are seen to be most important.
- Sport specific skills & knowledge (generally played at the same/similar level).
- Respect & empathy
- Good interpersonal skills
- Charismatic
- Consistency & fairness
- Clear vision & goals.
- Motivated & enthusiastic

LAISSEZ-FAIRE

- Little direction or decisions made by the leader.
- Often made by the team.
- Not seen in action too much, though some aspects can increase motivation - feel they can be trusted. Will only work with an experienced group.

EMERGENT

- Emerges from within the group/team
- Selected by their peers due to their leadership character-istics. eg the next team captain.
- Generally the most successful leaders, as they have the support & respect of the team.
- However, they may not view aspects of the game objectively (or the team), leading to bias in selection due to friendship groups.

Or...

PRESCRIBED

- Selected for the position by an external body eg senior committee at a rugby club appoint from outside the organisation.
- Usually done when an 'overhaul' or change is needed within the set up.
- Has the advantage of coming in with fresh ideas & an unbiased view.
- ...however, group cohesion may suffer in the short term, due to unfamiliarity with the team culture & new working relationships.

Leaders can be...

70

CHELLADURI'S MODEL OF LEADERSHIP

LEADER CHARACTERISTICS

- Refers to how experienced the leader is & the **personality** of the leader.
- i.e. has the leader got the experience to deal with a group in a dangerous situation?

ACTUAL BEHAVIOUR considers what the leader actually decides to do.

- e.g. a more **autocratic** style as an experienced leader would increase trust from the group, as they know it is of benefit to listen to the leader.

MEMBER CHARACTERISTICS

- Refers to the **age & experience** of the group. i.e. a group of 10yr old students will generally be inexperienced in more dangerous activities.

PREFERRED BEHAVIOUR refers to the **style** of leadership favoured by the group. Continuing with the theme of dangerous activities, the group would prefer a more **autocratic** style of leadership, as the leader is telling them exactly what to do & they feel safe with this.

* If required, preferred & actual behaviour match, both performance & satisfaction increases.

MULTI-DIMENSIONAL MODEL

CHELLADURI (1990) identified **3** variables or antecedents that influence leadership. They are...

SITUATIONAL CHARACTERISTICS

- Environmental circumstances i.e. is the activity dangerous?

REQUIRED BEHAVIOUR refers to the most suitable behaviours by the leader.
- i.e. is the leader experienced in the size of a group, tasks etc.
- In the case of the activity being dangerous, an autocratic leadership style would be best suited.

- SITUATIONAL CHARACTERISTICS
- LEADER CHARACTERISTICS
- MEMBER CHARACTERISTICS

To assess the effectiveness of leadership, behaviours must be analysed. *

CONSEQUENCES

7. Performance

Satisfaction.

LEADER BEHAVIOUR

4. Required Behaviours
5. Actual Behaviours
6. Preferred Behaviours

ANTECEDENTS

1. Situational Characteristics
2. Leader Characteristics
3. Member Characteristics

* If required & actual behaviour match, performance increases.

* If preferred & actual behaviour match, satisfaction increases.

THEORIES OF LEADERSHIP

FIEDLER'S CONTINGENCY MODEL & THEORIES

TRAIT PERSPECTIVE
- Leadership qualities are innate & genetically inherited.
- You either a born leader or not.' (NATURE).
- The early thinking behind the instinct theory was called 'THE GREAT MAN THEORY', where leaders are men as they are born with the relevant personality traits to be an effective leader.
- However, this theory fails to take into account any situational, environmental & interaction factors.

SITUATIONAL VARIABLES
LEADERSHIP STYLES

RELATIONSHIP BETWEEN STYLES & SITUATION

SOCIAL LEARNING
- Leadership qualities are learnt from others through observation & modelling (NURTURE).
- This learning process is strengthened if it is observed from a significant other (someone the person respects or someone of a higher status).

INTERACTIONIST
- Possess certain innate leadership traits, but only demonstrate these in specific (state) situations.
- Interaction of traits & dynamic environment.

FIEDLER (1967)
FIEDLER (1967) identified 2 styles of leadership...
- TASK ORIENTATED
- PERSON ORIENTATED

TASK ORIENTATED
- This style of leadership is concerned about achieving a particular outcome i.e. winning.
- There are clear goals.
- Would suit a more autocratic leader.
- Generally has the greatest success in the most & least favourable scenarios.

PERSON ORIENTATED
- Concerned with the personal relationships & building strong (group) cohesion.
- Generally works with a more experienced group where a more democratic leader would be suitable & where opinions are valued.
- This leadership style has most success in moderately favourable scenarios.

Topic 4: Sport Psychology

1. **Compare** the interactionalist perspective of learning to the trait theory of personality. *(6 marks)*

2. **Outline** the three components of attitude within the Wood's Triadic Model. *(3 marks)*

3. **Evaluate** the Drive Theory of arousal and its application with regards to achieving optimal sporting performance. *(8 marks)*

4. During a netball match, some players can become over-aroused and/or show signs of anxiety.
   With reference to the 'catastrophe theory', **describe** how over-arousal and anxiety can affect a player's performance. *(4 marks)*

5. Using examples, **describe** the difference between the three dimensions of anxiety. *(6 marks)*

6. **Outline** 3 cognitive stress management techniques that performers can use to reduce the negative effects of anxiety. *(3 marks)*

7. Rugby Union is a collision sport that can lead to aggressive behaviour.
   Use the aggressive-cue hypothesis to **explain** how this might occur. *(3 marks)*

8. **Compare** the different types of aggression in sport. *(8 marks)*

9. **Suggest** strategies to reduce aggressive play. *(4 marks)*

10. **Explain** the two dimensions of Achievement Motivation. *(4 marks)*

11. **Examine** the effect that home advantage has on the performance of a home team. *(8 marks)*

12. **Identify** strategies to reduce social loafing. *(4 marks)*

13. **Describe** the difference between outcome and performance goals. *(2 marks)*

14. **Explain** how a coach could use Weiner's Attributional model to maintain and/or improve motivation after a loss? *(6marks)*

15. Bandura suggests there are 4 factors that affect a performer's self-efficacy. Using examples, **explain** the 4 factors. *(8 marks)*

16. **Analyse** the most appropriate leadership style(s) for coaching performers in the cognitive stage of learning. *(8 marks)*

<u>Total Marks:</u> /85

Topic S: Sport and Society

What you need to learn:		Yes	Nearly	No
S.1: The factors leading to the emergence and development of modern-day sport	S.1.1: Overview of the emergence and development of modern-day sport. The historical and social context of popular recreations: characteristics of mob activities (peasants) and those for the courtly/aristocracy in pre-industrial Britain — field sports, games and pastimes.			
	S.1.2: The effect of the Industrial Revolution on British society and how it was reflected in recreational activities. The impact on recreational activities leading from: industrialisation, urbanisation, education and transport developments.			
	S.1.3: The social cultural factors that influenced the development of rational recreation of sport in the post-industrial era. The role played by Thomas Arnold, Muscular Christianity and the cult of athleticism, the development of factory teams; the growth of the sporting press; establishment of the early national governing bodies (NGBs).			
	S.1.4: The emergence of competing for corporations rather than geographically-based teams; advantages and disadvantages.			

	S.1.5: Equality and diversity in disability sport and for gender, with specific reference to the ParaSport movement and improved opportunities for women in global sport.			
	S.1.6: Migration patterns of sporting labour and the impact on domestic competitions and national teams.			
S.2: Globalisation of sport	S.2.1: Overview of the concept of the 'globalisation of sport'; definition, features and the impacts on sport and society.			
	S.2.2: Colonial diffusion of sport across the British Empire; roles of the Army, Church, Industry and Education. Overview of the further creation and development of international sport.			
	S.2.3: The creation, development and impact of national and international governing bodies on sport and society.			
	S.2.4: The context and impact of participating at the Modern Olympic Games, World Cups, and major international sporting events. Exploration of the issues of bidding for, staging and competing at world events.			
S.3: Commercialisation of sport	S.3.1: Knowledge and understanding of the commercialisation of sport and its impact on society.			
	S.3.2: An understanding of the concept of commercialisation and commodities.			

	Comparisons between advertising, sponsorship, endorsement and merchandising.			
	S.3.3: The historical and social context of commercialisation: broken time payments; spectatorism; developments in the media.			
	S.3.4: The events of the 1968, 1972 and the 1976 Olympics and their impact on the 1984 games in Los Angeles. The blueprint for the commercialisation of future sport created by Peter Ueberroth at the 1984 Games.			
	S.3.5: Franchises in sport (USA and UK), the concept of the 'golden triangle'. Sports stars as global stars. The Americanisation of sport. The concept of competitive sports fixtures and events being played on other continents. For example, NFL, NBA, Tour de France.			
S.4: Ethics and deviance in sport	S.4.1: Knowledge and understanding of ethics and deviance in sport. The pressures on sports performers and spectators to behave in a deviant way.			
	S.4.2: The impact of commercialisation on the sportsmanship ethic and the growth of gamesmanship in the UK.			
	S.4.3: Deviance in sport: use of performance enhancing drugs, (early conception of drug use up to the modern			

	day); blood doping and transfusions; diuretics and pain relief; simulation; bribery; 'bungs'; match fixing, betting syndicates and other contemporary forms of deviance.			
	S.4.4: Different responses of national and international governing bodies, governments and the law to combat deviance in sport, including the utilisation of technology.			
	S.4.5: The role of the World Anti-doping Agency (WADA) in combating the use of performance enhancing drugs.			
S.5: The relationship between sport and the media	S.5.1: Knowledge and understanding of the two-way relationship between sport and the media. The development of media coverage from print to televised events and its role in sport. Reasons for the growth of live media/social media coverage and its implications for performers, supporters and the sport.			
	S.5.2: The impact of technology on the viewing experience. The advantages and disadvantages of the development of specific sports media packages and the growth of 'pay per view'.			

S.6: Development routes from talent identification through to elite performance	S.6.1: Knowledge and understanding of UK talent identification and development: novice to elite performer. The historical influences on UK provisions – East Germany and Australia.			
S.7: Participation and health of the nation	S.7.1: Knowledge and understanding of barriers to participation, the benefits of mass participation and the impact of wearable technology on participation.			
	S.7.2: Concept of mass participation and initiatives/programmes to promote community participation in the UK.			
	S.7.3: Participation trends in the UK in the 21st century.			

THE EMERGENCE AND DEVELOPMENT OF MODERN DAY SPORT

UPPER CLASS

- which included LANDOWNERS & the GENTRY, possessed the power & influence over what was a rural & feudal society.
- Had a lot of wealth & time to pursue their interests.
- They were educated & therefore activities contained more complex rules / laws & included...
  - Bar force / hunting
  - Falconry
  - Horse Racing
  - Archery
  - Croquet
  - Real tennis
- Cricket (though this became a 'mixed' social class sport with the upper classes looking to recruit strong fast bowlers).

FINALLY...

- The final section considers SPORT IN SOCIETY, from Pre-Industrial Britain, to the sport of today.

PRE-INDUSTRIAL BRITAIN

- Had a two class society with the ARISTOCRATS (upper class) participating in vastly different popular recreational activities than the PEASANTS (lower class).
- General characteristics of POPULAR RECREATION pre-industrial revolution include...
- Violent & cruel, a reflection on society at that time.
- Localised (village v village) due to lack of infrastructure & transport. Horse drawn courages the main mode of transport.
- Male dominated.
- Reliance on strength & power, not skill.
- Very few rules / unwritten rules (low literacy rates amongst peasants).
- Limited equipment
- Unstructured / uncodified
- no fixed playing area, time, participants.

MOB GAMES:
- played occasionally eg holy days, wakes etc
- Alcohol & wagering

LOWER CLASS

- Lived a SUBSISTENCE EXISTENCE
- Poor, labour or trade based jobs.
- Poor conditions, lived in basic cottages, no running water.
- Limited access to transport.
- Recreational pursuits included...
- Boxing / prize fighting
- Cock fighting / bear baiting
- Mob games: mob football
(eg shrovetide football - still played today in Ashbourne), Haxey Hood game.

Pre-Industrial | 1700 | 1800 | 1900 | 2000 | Post-Industrial

Popular Recreation

Public School Athleticism

Rational Recreation

State Elementary Education

THE EFFECT OF THE INDUSTRIAL REVOLUTION ON BRITISH SOCIETY

The focus here is to look at the impact of recreational activities leading from...

- industrialisation
- urbanisation
- education
- transport developments

THE INDUSTRIAL REVOLUTION

- Led to many changes in British society, including the development of sport.

- ... however, more specifically it refers to the move from an AGRARIAN ECONOMY (trade & the sale of crops & farmland), to an INDUSTRIAL SOCIETY (dominated by the manufacturing industry).

- This ultimately led to the URBANISATION of the country, where new towns & cities were created to cater for the new job opportunities.

- There were changes in society with regards to different jobs available & the way work was conducted with an increase of machinery.

- There was an increase in the number of factories (ie businesses making clothes, shoes & the creation of steam engines).

- With every increase in new businesses, society saw a rise of the MIDDLE CLASS (managers of factories & other businesses).

URBANISATION

- There was a migration of people from land (countryside) to the new towns that had been created, offering greater employment prospects for the lower classes.

- Initially the conditions were poor, very poor.

- The lower classes had to work long hours for little pay & lived in urban slums.

- Due to the long working hours, there was little time for the working class to play sport.

- A lot of disease & malnutrition (from poor conditions & low wages) prevented full participation.

- The development of towns meant that there were less open spaces, so activities still reflected 'small games' outside of urbanised areas in the early stages of industrial revolution.

WHAT WAS IT LIKE?

If you are trying to picture what it may have been like, think about the opening ceremony of London 2012, where the 'green & pleasant lands' are turned into smouldering landscapes covered with factories, mills & chimneys.

81

SPORTING EVOLUTION

- As England became more **industrialised & urbanised** (mid 1800s) sport became more **RATIONAL** (organised, **codified**, more regular).
- **Transport links** through improvements in roads, waterways & railways allowed for more fixtures & **further afield** visits increased
- **spectators**
- **factory teams** were developed & influenced by the **middle class** as they realised the positive physical & mental impact of healthier employees & the increase in moral within their businesses.
- **Fair play** was encouraged.
- Specific facilities were purposely built, to accommodate fixtures. This was also influenced by the lack of space in townships & the need for some kind of town planning.
- Towards the end of the 1800s, working conditions improved as a result of the Industrial Relations Act (1871). shorter working days and a ½ day on a Saturday increased **opportunities to participate in sport (for the working classes)**. This was the start of the **BRITISH SPORTING SATURDAY AFTERNOON.**
- Gambling was still evident, though with greater controls.

THE EFFECT OF THE INDUSTRIAL REVOLUTION ON BRITISH SOCIETY

TRANSPORT

- Better transport (through the increase of steam powered rail travel), meant **fixtures** could be played in more regional areas, ultimately leading to the creation of leagues & competitions.

- With better transport, **spectatorism** increased.
- factory owners would arrange excursions to the coast in an attempt to boost morale (& productivity!)
- local improvements meant cycling became increasingly popular - developing as a sport.

EDUCATION

- In the 1700s, only the sons of wealthy families went to school, with girls being home schooled.
- As a result, most children could not read or write & literacy levels were low.
- In the early 1800s, most **middle & upper class boys** went to school, but very few **lower class** boys.
- By the end of the 1800s, high schools/state schools were opened in major towns & cities, though education was still dominated by the **upper & middle classes** in **PUBLIC (PRIVATE) SCHOOLS.**
- There was evidence of **RATIONAL RECREATION** or 'more organised' sport in & between the different schools.
- ...though there was still a big gap to the **lower classes** who had **no formal education** & still participated in popular & unstructured recreation.

DEVELOPMENT OF FACTORY TEAMS

- As sports clubs, teams & leagues started to develop, some businesses & factories began to form teams aswell.

- Many teams have their roots from local pubs, churches, workers unions, company/factory teams.

- Eg West Bromwich Albion was founded in 1879 as the West Bromwich Strollers - the company team of Salter's Spring works, located in Birmingham.

- Factory owners saw the benefits to their business with regards to morale & the ever increasing press coverage.

- The working class were also interested in how event entertainment, the sense of accomplishment & camaraderie for their newly formed friends, colleagues & team mates.

RATIONAL RECREATION OF SPORT IN THE POST INDUSTRIAL ERA

Focussing on :....
- Thomas Arnold
- Muscular Christianity
- The cult of athleticism
- Factory teams
- The sporting press
- Early NGB's

- Future churchmen were former public-school boys & used sport as a way of guiding the youth into making good life decisions in line with their religious beliefs.

THE CHURCH

- For centuries festivals had involved the church & it was a way of getting people together to celebrate various events. eg fairs, feast days, wakes.

- During these events it was popular to include the various recreations of the time, such as mob football.

- ... however many clergymen tried to stop these activities as they saw these (working class activities) as immoral as they often involved drinking alcohol, gambling & were violent in nature.

- Sometimes men would visit other parishes in another locality where attitudes were not as strict in an attempt to participate.

- As sport became more (rational), the attitudes of the church started to change as they saw the benefits of channelling their energy into achieving a common goal with their peers.

RATIONAL RECREATION OF SPORT IN THE POST INDUSTRIAL ERA

ESTABLISHMENT OF EARLY NGB's

- NGB's? National Governing Bodies.

- The next stage in the develop-ment of rational sport was competing against other Public Schools.

- Initially this was problematic as all schools had their own localised rules. Matches were often played with an agreement on rules prior to kick off.

- CODIFICATION or standardisation of the laws/rules of game activities was mainly driven by former public schoolboys who attended the two major universities (of the time) in Oxford & Cambridge, known as the OXBRIDGE MELTING POT.

- This was seen as the first establish-ment of an NGB.

- From here, the creation of other NGB's occurred through discussion with the Oxbridge, such as the FA (1863) & the RFU (1871) - major NGB's today!

- Games were now more accessible to the general population with an increase in leagues across the country.

- Sport had now become a major aspect of everyday life, with clear moral values associated. Gone was the 'mob culture!'

- 'THE ENGLISH GAME' on Netflix gives a great insight into all these issues!

GROWTH OF THE SPORTING PRESS

- Advancements in the rail network, as well as technological advancements in the telegraph system led to an expansion in newspaper production.

- The improvements in educational standards further improved literacy & reading skills, now allowed people of all classes to understand the written content.

- Living standards were progressively improving. Middle class families had more 'disposable income' & greater 'leisure time', to either play sport or be a spectator.

- This in turn lead to an increase in sports journalism in the 19th century, offering free publicity to players, teams, factories & businesses and leagues.

The stories & reports published in the papers (with a new column just for sport), stimulated an increase in sport participation & spectatorship, especially with lower-class sports like football.

MUSCULAR CHRISTIANITY, SOCIAL CONTROL AND ATHLETICISM

- **THOMAS ARNOLD**, Headmaster of Rugby School (1820-1842) did not like the unruly behaviour of the boys, but was also not a strong believer in harsh punishment.

- He was not totally fond of games activities either, but he could see the benefits for the boys at school.

- In order to develop the qualities required of the sons of the gentry, he set about a series of reforms to bring about **social control**.

- He believed in giving students some responsibility & developing strong Christian morals through traditional principles.

- One way he encouraged this was to allow both farmers & prefects to stay in his cottage in the Lake District.

- As a reward for acting as good Christian role models, the boys were given more power & higher status within the school. The amount of organised house sport was increased to keep the boys occupied during their free time.

- This **refers** to the notion of **ATHLETICISM** & a way of promoting **MUSCULAR CHRISTIANITY** into the ethos of British public schoolboys.

PUBLIC SCHOOLS (centre)

THEIR ROLE
- In the 19th century, public schools were very elitist & exclusive for the upper class due to the high fees.
- Most students boarded, as their families lived too far away in the country.
- Conditions were surprisingly poor due to...
  - Basic living conditions, no hot water, basic accommodation & uninspiring food.
  - Strict discipline/harsh treatment, including beatings!
  - Bullying & fagging (made to do chores) for older boys - institutional through prefects & house system.
  - Limited supervision, so rowdy & unruly recreations.

THE CLARENDON COMMISSION
- Established in 1861.
- To investigate the conditions of 9 Public Schools with regards finance, management & infrastructure.
- Including: Eton, Rugby, Charterhouse, Shrewsbury, Winchester, Westminster, Harrow, Merchant Taylors' & St Paul's.
- Report was published in 1864, & made recommendations around curriculum, governance & issues around bullying & fagging.
- The report highlighted the positive impact team games had on the lives of the students in terms of training good character & improving individual & group morals.

- The newly formed manly & acceptable way of exercising promoted the values that society was looking for, such as...
  - loyalty.
  - fair play.
  - integrity.
  - dignity in defeat.

CORPORATION TEAMS

ADVANTAGES

- More money (potentially) for the team / franchise to buy better players.
- Greater exposure through TV, social media & merchandise to advertise their companies / corporation in an attempt to increase profits.
- Supporters can associate an image of the club or certain players without any connection to a geographical location (eg Manchester United have big followings in the USA & Asia, the LA Lakers in Asia also).
- Corporations can sponsor teams with no national ties. eg Lewis Hamilton is the lead driver / face of the F1 team Mercedes & has sponsors from Malaysia (Petronas), the USA (Tommy Hilfiger) & Switzerland (UBS) amongst others.

DISADVANTAGES

- No national or local identity that binds the players & wider clubs together.
- Lack of enthusiasm from fans compared to the passion they show when supporting the national team.
- The richest corporations can make it hard for emerging teams to progress (unable to afford top players).
- If the corporation decides to withdraw their funding, it could leave the team in financial difficulty.
- Decisions could be based on finance or for business reasons rather than maintaining a 'community club' ethos.

A CORPORATION

- Is a large company or group of companies that provide financial investment into a sporting team or franchise, that generally have (or are in pursuit of) global appeal.
  eg Red Bull in Formula One. 'Team Ineos' (formerly 'Team Sky') in cycling.
- Performers compete for corporations rather than geographically based teams.
  eg In the Japanese Top League (Rugby Union), players are contracted to a company - eg Panasonic Wild Knights.
- Corporations use the elite sporting platform to invest into major sports, expanding their portfolio, knowing the exposure some sports (especially football) get on TV & social media.
- eg 40% of Premier League clubs are majority owned by people / companies not UK based & 35% have additional investment.

WOMEN IN SPORT

THE WOMEN'S SPORTS FOUNDATION

- The struggle of challenging stereotypes & providing opportunities for women has been a big challenge (& still is!)
- The WSF, established in 1974, has helped to advance the lives of women & girls through sport & physical activity.
- The WSF provides financial support for aspiring athletes & educational programmes to help get girls more active. Eg Sports for Life & Athlete Ambassador Programmes.

WSF

HISTORICALLY

- Women were banned from playing sport as it was deemed too rough & violent and that only men had the strength & power to overcome such challenges.
- Not included in the first Olympics (1896).

Reasons

- for not participating in sport/physical activity can be due to time, cost, social class or transport issues.
- however, as previously mentioned, many of these issues were addressed during the development of sport during the Industrial Revolution.
- Nevertheless, some of these issues continued historically & certain sections have been excluded or discriminated against with regards to sports participation, including...
  - People with disabilities
  - women
  - ethnic minorities.
  - older people.
- Although there is still a long way to go with regards to opportunities for women's sport to be in line with their male counterparts, great strides have been made in the last 15 years. There is greater exposure of elite women's sport on TV, especially with Sky Sports (helping to fund further investment).

Examples include

- Netball Superleague established 2005. All players paid a salary (£18,200 minimum 2021)
- England Rugby squad fully professional from January 2019.
- ECB - 2014, 14 central contracts to 18 players. 2021 - figure now 41.
- FA WSL started in 2011. New TV deal - BBC & Sky.

EQUAL PAY

- Continues to be debated. However as sportspeople are now commodities, the market ultimately determines the value.
- Tennis (a fairly equal sport in terms of participation) has seen equal pay for tournament winners of respective genders.
- Since 2007, men & women's single winners get the same payment. Is this fair? In favour of women? Men play 5 set matches, women just 3!?

DISABILITY SPORT

DISABILITY SPORT

- During the 1948 London Olympics, Dr Guttman organised the first competition for wheelchair athletes, involving 16 injured servicemen & women (taking part in archery).
- Called the Stoke Mandeville Games (after the hospital), but later renamed the PARALYMPIC GAMES. This was first held in Rome in 1960 & featured 400 athletes from 23 countries.
- This was part of Dr. Guttman's new approach to rehabilitation for injuries obtained in WWII & centred around sport.
- The first Winter Games Paralympics was in Sweden in 1976.
- Both Summer & Winter Games were held separately from the 'able bodied' Games until Seoul, South Korea (1988) & Albertville, France (1992) for the Summer & Winter Games respectively.
- The 'Para Games' now take place in the same cities & venues as the Olympics, with the main turning point for mainstream coverage being London 2012.

ACTIVITY ALLIANCE

- Formerly known as the English Federation of Disability Sport, established in 1998 & is the leading voice for disabled people in sport.
- They recognise disabled people are twice as likely to be inactive. Aim - close the gap within a generation. How? - change people's attitudes towards disabled people in sport.
- Work closely with other organisations, such as UK Deaf Sport & British Blind Sport.

2013

- The Duke of Sussex 'Prince' Harry visited the Warrior Games in the USA & witnessed how the power of sport could help those suffering from injuries, physically, socially & psychologically.
- This led to the development of the INVICTUS GAMES, used to inspire recovery, support rehabilitation & integrate ex-servicemen & women back into society.
- INVICTUS means unconquered, which seems very appropriate in defining the fighting spirit of wounded athletes.

PARASPORT

- Movement developed by ParalympicsGB in partnership with Toyota as part of their commitment to making the movement better for everyone.
- Why? To create the biggest UK wide community for players, parents & coaches to share experiences, tips & hints.

MIGRATION PATTERNS OF SPORTING LABOUR

MIGRATION

- Migration of sporting labour refers to the movement of performers from one country or continent to another to pursue their career.

- Due to the impact of increased professionalism, globalisation & commercialisation of sport, certain performers have a higher market value than others in other parts of the world.

- The rise of certain sports or events, such as 20:20 cricket, has seen some cricketers living a nomadic migratory lifestyle going from one 20:20 tournament to the next (eg Chris Gayle playing in the Indian IPL, the Australian Big Bash & the West Indian Twenty 20 and so on).

- Increased media coverage has led to higher contracts, lucrative sponsorship deals & more wealthy overseas investors providing increased funds, hence the movement.

DISADVANTAGES

- Player drain from domestic competition as players move for more lucrative deals abroad. This then...

- Puts pressure on selection decisions for national teams & effective competition for places in domestic leagues. eg rugby players from around the world sign big contracts in Japan/France towards the end of their career.

- 12.5% of the GB team for London 2012 were born outside the UK & were dubbed

PLASTIC BRITS - only using their British nationality to enhance their career.

- eg Sprint hurdler Tiffany Porter was born & raised in the USA, has a British passport (mother). People said she chose to represent Team GB as not good enough for the USA team!

- Overseas players inhibiting opportunities for home grown talent to develop & shine. eg 2019/20 the Premier League only had 37% domestic players, compared to 60% in La Liga. This is the lowest of the big European Leagues (eg Ligue 1, Bundesliga etc).

- 'Lack of knowledge' regarding tradition & ideals. eg 'foreign players bringing diving in to English football. This did not sit well with the fans.

Non-selection of players for international games if they play overseas. eg to play for England at rugby, the players must play 'domestically'.

ADVANTAGES

- Improved standard of domestic competition. eg Premier League.

- Improved standards due to foreign coaches.

- Increased commercial investment, by better players.

- Opportunity to play at international level. eg 6 Nations - Scotland had 15 foreign born players in 2021.

89

CREATION & DEVELOPMENT OF INTERNATIONAL SPORT

FIRST KNOWN INTERNATIONAL FIXTURES

1844 - First international cricket match. USA v Canada at St. George's Cricket Club, New York.

1859 - First team of English Professional cricketers visited North America for the first overseas tour.

1862 - The first English cricket team toured Australia.

1868 - The first Australian cricket team toured England (made solely of Aboriginal people).

1871 - First international rugby fixture between Scotland & England at Raeburn Place, Edinburgh.

1872 - First international football match between Scotland & England at the west of Scotland cricket ground.

1877 - First cricket test match between England & Australia at the MCG.

1882 - First Ashes test match between England & Australia at the Oval, London.

1896 - First modern Olympic Games in Athens.

1930 - First football World Cup held in Uruguay (won by Uruguay who beat Argentina 4-2).

1930 - First Commonwealth Games held in Hamilton, Canada. Originally called the British Empire Games. (11 countries in attendance).

1954 - First rugby league World Cup held in France, with Great Britain beating France 16-12 in the final.

1963 - First netball World Cup in Eastbourne, England. Australia beat New Zealand by one point in the final.

1971 - First men's hockey World Cup held in Barcelona, Spain, won by Pakistan.

1974 - First women's hockey World Cup, held in France, won by the Netherlands.

1975 - First cricket World Cup held in England, with the West Indies beating Australia by 17 runs.

1983 - First World Athletics Championships held in Helsinki, Finland.

1987 - First rugby union world Cup held in New Zealand & Australia. NZ beat France 29-9 in the final.

1995 - First professional rugby by union World Cup in South Africa.

SPORT

- Became a tool for developing social cohesion & ensuring status in society between newly formed communities & indigenous people.

- As the colonised communities became more developed, the population kept a lot of the traditions & sport that had been introduced, soon developing governing bodies.

- Schools also played a big part in the development of sport as the schools systems were based on the same principles as Public Schools in England.

90

COLONIAL DIFFUSION OF SPORT

- Occurred across the British Empire.

- The clergy controlled sport to a certain extent in Britain & parishes used it as a way of revolutionising students as well as having clear links with **Public Schools**.

- **The Church** also set up colonies where their work would include teaching sport to the indigenous population eg Africa.

- With all visits to the colonial nations, the Army played a big part in diffusing sport in the new nation.

- Military personnel had to stay in shape through daily physical training.

- In addition the organisation of inter-unit sport was implemented to maintain regiment morale. This led to the involvement of the locals.

- Through the 'old boy system', returning expats (often Oxbridge graduates) became House & Sports Masters, reinforcing sporting values.

- The same system was used for new colonies. Schools were created & the educators would educate newly settled & military children, as well as introducing the games to the local indigenous population.

The IMPACT & INFLUENCE of the British Empire can still be seen today in countries that were previously were colonies.

GLOBALISATION OF SPORT

CRICKET - South Africa, New Zealand, Australia, India, Pakistan, Bangladesh, Zimbabwe, the West Indies.

RUGBY - South Africa, New Zealand, Australia, Canada.

NETBALL - South Africa, New Zealand, Australia, Jamaica.

TENNIS - various colonised nations.

GLOBALISATION

- Refers to the network of interdependencies across the globe that view sport as a business.

- To make this a success, corporate investment, media coverage, sponsorship & the freedom of movement of performers, coaching staff, officials & spectators is required. *Hugely difficult currently due to the (2020 Coronavirus pandemic - 21).

- Positive aspects include the learning of new skills & cultures to enhance performance that would not be learnt if the performer stayed in his/her own country, as well as providing the opportunity to perform on the world stage with greater fame, exposure & more money.

- Negative aspects could include... the loss of national identity, loss of talent from less developed nations to more powerful nations on the global stage. eg Pacific Island rugby players often go to New Zealand to progress their career further & earn more money.

NATIONAL & INTERNATIONAL GOVERNING BODIES

ROLES OF NGB's

- Promote & develop their sport through various initiatives & programmes. e.g Walking netball/football – led to an increase in participation & activity rates.
- Target performers at all levels of participation.
- Introduction, modification & enforcement of rules.
- Organisation of competitions, leagues & cups.
- Liaison with other agencies & International Governing Bodies (IGB's).

NGB FUNDING

NGB's receive money through the following avenues...

- Club affiliation fees.
- Sport England funding.
- National lottery grants.
- UK Sport funding.
- Sponsorship.
- TV deals.

PROFESSIONAL SPORTS

... such as football (the FA), rugby union & league (the RFU & RFL) & cricket (the ECB) tend to get most of their funding through TV deals & Sponsorship.

AS PREVIOUSLY

- mentioned, it was the 'Old Boys' from the Oxbridge Universities who created the first governing bodies that provided/sports with a set of codified laws, rules & regulations.
- The vast majority of NGB's were established in the latter years of the 1800s & were initially developed with the view of recreation (that was amateur), instead of being created for professional purposes.
- NGB's were based on a decentralised model where local associations were self-governing.
- ... however most NGB's are based on a centralised model today where rules, initiatives & procedures come from a central hub & all county and local associations apply them.
- This development led to NGB's as we know them today, such as the FA ... the FOOTBALL ASSOCIATION.

OLYMPIC SPORTS

... NGB's like rowing (British Rowing), cycling (British Cycling) & badminton (BADMINTON ENGLAND) receive a lot/most of their funding from UK Sport every 4 years, based on their performance at the previous Olympic Games.

IGB's

- The first known IGB was the **BUREAU OF EUROPEAN GYMNASTICS FEDERATIONS**, formed in 1881 & became the **INTERNATIONAL GYMNASTICS FEDERATION** 40 years later.

- The best known IGB is the **IOC**; the **INTERNATIONAL OLYMPIC COMMITTEE**, established in Paris in 1894. A not-for-profit independent organisation, the **IOC** is now based in Lausanne (Switzerland). It is privately funded & distributes 90% of it's revenue to the development of sport & athletes of all levels.

- There are **many, many** more IGB's, with examples including...

FIBA - International Basketball Federation.

FIFA - Federation Internationale de Football Association.

IAAF - International Association of Athletics Federations.

ICC - International Cricket Council.

BWF - Badminton World Federation.

INTERNATIONAL GOVERNING BODIES

FINA - Federation Internationale de Natation (Swimming).

INF - International Netball Federation.

UEFA - Union of European Football Associations.

<u>Not</u> an IGB, but is one of six continental confederations of FIFA. **UEFA** consists of 55 national association members from the **FA's** of Europe. They run national/club competitions (Champions League, Europa League & 'the Euros').

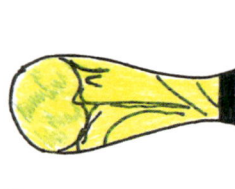

ROLE OF IGB's

- Work with other sporting organisations and **NGB's** from other countries with regard to rule change proposals.

- Update on developments of required facilities & equipment requirements (for competition).

- Establish safeguarding initiatives.

- Work with other countries & **WADA (WORLD ANTI-DOPING AGENCY)** to consolidate anti-doping rules, sanctions and educational programmes.

- Provide information regarding coaching & officiating the game.

- Play a major role in establishing an international calendar of events including the scheduling and organisation of World Cups & major international tournaments.

- work with **NGB's** in promoting the sport on a global stage.

THE OLYMPIC CREED

- Has been on the score board during the opening ceremony at each Modern Olympic Games.

'The most important thing is not to win but to take part, just as the most important thing in life is not the triumph, but the struggle. The essential thing is not to have conquered, but to have fought well.'

Pierre de Coubertin

(Olympic rings symbol)

FIRST GAMES

- 1896 in Athens.
- 5 days, 9 sports, 32 events, 311 athletes ... but 0 women! That was in Paris in 1900.

PIERRE DE COUBERTIN

- Baron Pierre de Coubertin can be credited as the 'founder' of the modern day Olympic movement.

- He developed the ideals surrounding the modern Olympic Games, with the idea of OLYMPISM becoming clear in the Olympic Charter as...

'... a philosophy of life, exalting & combining in a balanced whole the qualities of body, will and mind. Blending sport with culture and education, Olympism seeks to create a way of life based on the joy of effort, the educational value of good example, social responsibility and respect for universal fundamental ethical principles.'

THE MODERN OLYMPIC GAMES

De Coubertin wanted to 'revive' the Ancient Olympic Games 'ideal' & inspired by the Much Wenlock Games in Shropshire, set about doing so...

AIM OF OLYMPISM

- Is to demonstrate how sport can help foster better relationships between communities & nations, helping us to live in harmony with one another.

-This is one of the reasons why countries (specifically cities) bid to host major sporting events like the Olympics (& World Cups, Commonwealth Games etc).

- It is a way to support local communities with the development of better infrastructure, as well as massive financial gain (spectators, tourism).

- However, there are issues... (P96).

OLYMPIC VALUES

- EXCELLENCE
- FRIENDSHIP
- RESPECT

Potential Benefits of Hosting Major Games

- Increase in national pride (especially if the team/country does well).

- Raise the status of the country. Eyes of the world on a country/city for the duration of the Olympics or World Cup. Want to look good, no trouble, great facilities, welcoming.

- This puts the country/city in the 'shop window' to promote the country's culture & status on the world stage.

- In turn this may lead to an increase in tourism either...
  - Directly - coming to watch games/event at the host city.
  - Indirectly - visiting afterwards, or to other parts of the country. Economic benefits at local &/or national level.

- Jobs created as a result of the event, facilities built & the increase in tourism.

- Increased commercialism from sponsors (international, national & local). 'New' money only as a result of the event.

- Better community facilities & transport links (infrastructure) as a result. eg Javelin train into central London, new roads, train station.

- Strengthens ruling political party in charge.

- Increase in commercial interest in certain sports.

- Unity amongst the population. 'Want to do well.' Increase in morale, a 'feel good factor'. eg London 2012, 'Super Saturday.'

- The event can raise the profile of the sport & may lead to an increase in participation. Spectators see role models doing well & want to copy them. eg Women's Football World Cup, 2015. Can create a sporting legacy.

- New facilities or upgraded venues. eg London stadium, aquatics centre, velodrome (but at a cost)

- Olympic villages & accommodation create new communities. eg Athletes village in Stratford converted into social housing.

- Greater focus on 'minority sports' in the Olympics, allows people to understand different activities that may inspire them to participate.

- Increased funding for sport.

- list
- link

POTENTIAL DRAWBACKS OF HOSTING MAJOR GAMES

- Ticket prices are often too expensive for the local population.

EXPLOITED

- Some employment opportunities (building stadia, infrastructure) are only short lived.

- Certain countries may not have great reputations with regard to human rights, ideology & the treatment of migrant workers. eg Qatar

Football World Cup. More than 6,500 workers have died working on new stadia builds & homosexuality is illegal.

- Local people forced to move from land/houses being used in construction of venues.

Compulsory purchase orders often used if refuse. eg certain areas of London had to relocate people prior to 2012 & this was also seen in Beijing prior to 2008 & Rio de Janeiro prior to 2016.

- The cost of bidding is very expensive, even if you lose! eg Madrid failed in their bid for the 2016 Olympics at a cost of £34.7 million! The process was simplified in 2019 - now cheaper!!

- Negative impact on the economy during times of recession, or if too much money invested into the project that was not successful. eg Tokyo 2020 (21), economic impact of no overseas spectators.

- Facilities - if poorly organised & run, they could end up being left unused & derelict afterwards. eg Athens 2004, Beijing 2008.

- Acts of deviance highlighted by the media on a global stage. eg drug taking, hooliganism.

- Minority sports suffering from a loss of funding post Olympics due to poor performance. eg UK Sport withdrew the funding for volleyball after the London 2012 Olympics. Rowing post Tokyo 2020?

- Major issues such as protests and/or terrorist attacks (eg Munich 1972) could affect the country negatively + extra security costs.

- May cost more to host than can generate. eg Montreal 1976 Olympics left debts of $1.3 billion. Finally paid off in 2006! 30 years later & cost $2.5 billion.

THE GOLDEN TRIANGLE

- Encompasses the commercialised model, where all aspects (sport, media & sponsorship) are inter-linked to create a successful & financial product. (More on P103).

COMMERCIALISATION OF SPORT

COMMERCIALISATION

- 'Refers to how all aspects of sport are treated as a COMMODITY (a product that has a value), where players can be bought & sold, depending on their market value that is influenced by the media, endorsements & sponsorship.

ADVERTISING

- Sport is used to promote goods or services in order to improve sales & market business.
- In 2020, 148.5 million viewers watched the Super Bowl (figures were down in 2021).
- Due to the massive audience, the cost to advertise during the intervals/breaks has increased.
- Cost in 2020 for a 30 second commercial on Fox... a reported $5.6 million (up from $5.2 million in 2019).

SPONSORSHIP

- 'Providing funds or other forms of support to an individual or event in return for some commercial return.'
- eg Roger Federer signed a 10-year deal with Japanese clothing brand Uniqlo worth a reported $300 million over 10 years.

ENDORSEMENT

- 'Giving approval to a product or service & receiving payment in return.'
- eg Serena Williams has earned $93,634,967 in prize money over her career
- ... however, she also has an estimated net worth of $225 million from multiple endorsements with the likes of Nike, Gatorade, Wilson, Delta Air, Pepsi & Aston Martin (to name a few).

MERCHANDISING

- 'the use of a brand or image from a product is used to sell another.'
- ie the sale of sports shirts to promote a player or team.
- eg In 1984, Michael Jordan was a 21 yr old rookie who signed a 5 year deal with Nike worth $500,000 per year.
- This was substantially more than established players (like Magic Johnson - $300,000 per year from Converse).
- Nike also agreed to give Jordan his signature line. (Reportedly ... Air Jordan earned $3.14 billion in 2019).
- More recently Cristiano Ronaldo has become a member of a trio in the 'Nike billion dollar club', having signed a lifetime deal with Nike worth upwards of $1 billion! (The other 2 members are Michael Jordan & LeBron James). Nike see how much money Ronaldo makes them so have secured a long term deal.

COMMERCIALISATION - HISTORICALLY & SOCIALLY

SPECTATORISM

- An increase in free time, or 'leisure time' in the latter part of the 1800s gave rise not only to an increase in participation in sport, but also to a rise in SPECTATORISM.

- As a result of more spectators at games, businesses saw a good opportunity to start advertising & promoting their goods/services.

- This lead to an increase in SPONSORSHIP.

BROKEN-TIME PAYMENTS

- With added investment & Spectators now paying to watch sport, both the crowd & investors expected better quality of play.

- This put pressure on the young labour force to commit more time to training, travelling & playing.

- However, they were not initially compensated for the loss of time from work.

BROKEN-TIME PAYMENTS

- were introduced which upset the middle class clubs & authorities (mainly in the south of England).

- Football was first to introduce such payments, followed closely by the Northern Rugby Union. This led to a split between the RFU & NRU in 1893 & in 1897 the first Challenge Cup final was held at Headingley (Batley v St. Helens won 10-3 by Batley) watched by c. 13,000 fans.

- from 1895-1908 significant rule changes were made & rugby league was born. A different game to rugby & it also became more professional.

- Although some top players were getting their share of the 'pot', these underhand dealings became known as 'SHAMATEURISM' & an IRB working party reported that breaches of the amateur regulations were wholesale in March 1995.

- For another 99 years & 364 days, rugby union stayed in 'amateur mode'.

- In August 1995, during an RFU meeting in Paris, the International Board allowed the game to become more professional.

- The IRB did not really have a choice. So much money was now flowing into the game through advertising, TV & media coverage, it was an injustice players were not able to share the earnings.

IMPACT OF EVENTS AT THE OLYMPICS

THE IOC

- The International Olympic Committee aims to promote competitive sport... 'in a spirit of friendship, solidarity & fairplay.' However certain political events have disrupted the Games through boycotts, protests, terrorism etc...

1972 - MUNICH

MUNICH MASSACRE.

- Eight Palestinian terrorists affiliated with the **BLACK SEPTEMBER ORGANISATION** entered the Olympic Village, killing two members of the Israeli Olympic team & took nine others hostage in attempt to get 200 Palestinian prisoners released.

- Munich at the time was part of West Germany & the country wanted to show the world how far the country had developed & the relaxed nature of the police since the 1936 Berlin (Nazi) Games. As a result, heavy security was not a top priority.

- Plans to rescue the athletes were covered on TV & seen by the terrorists!

- German police were inadequately trained & equipped & failed in their ambush attempt at the airport. As a result, all nine Israeli hostages, five Palestinian terrorists & one policeman died.

1968 - MEXICO CITY

CIVIL RIGHTS PROTEST
- BLACK POWER
2 major political events...

1- 10 days before the opening ceremony, Mexican students protested at the use of government funding for the Olympics rather than using it to support socio-economic issues within the country. The Mexican Army surrounded the protestors & opened fire, killing over 200 people & injuring more than 1000.

2- Peter Norman, the Australian (who came 2nd in the 200m sprint), supported the Human Rights movement & wore a small badge that read 'Olympic Project for Human Rights' on his jacket (borrowed from an American rower.)

- He also suggested to both African American USA sprinters **Tommie Smith** & **John Carlos** (who finished 1st & 3rd respectively) to wear one black glove each for their **BLACK POWER SALUTE**.

- The pair raised their fists & bowed their heads during the USA national anthem in support of the civil rights movement. This ultimately led to an IOC & USAOC ban for the pair.

IMPACT OF EVENTS AT THE OLYMPICS

1984 - LOS ANGELES
THE 'HAMBURGER' GAMES.

- The lead up to the Games in LA was marred by political fallouts.

- Moscow 1980. The USA boycotted these games due to the invasion of Afghanistan in December 1979.
The result...
- This led to a 'tit for tat' boycott of the LA Games by the USSR & 'Eastern Bloc' countries eg East Germany.
- The state government were not in favour of funding the Olympics due to financial & political disasters from previous years.

- Local businessman Peter Ueberroth proposed what would become the first privately funded Olympics by forming a committee called 'LA84'.

- LA84 acted more like a corporation & was formed by entrepreneurs & other financial leaders. Corporate sponsorships, private fundraising & TV rights ($£225$ million) were used to fund the Olympics.

- McDonald's implemented a nationwide promotion, offering free Big Macs, fries & Cokes every time a US athlete reached the medals podium. This backfired (slightly) as with the USSR team boycotting, the US went on a winning streak.

- The LA84 committee saved money by not allowing new structures to be built. Stadia were modified & upgraded. eg 1932 Olympic stadium.

- LA84 made a deal. If the Games were profitable, 60% would go to USOC & 40% kept for Southern California. This was a good deal for both parties! Expenditure was $546 million, but surplus profit $232.5 million. Blueprint!

1976 - MONTREAL
AFRICAN COUNTRIES BOYCOTT.

- 22 countries from Africa boycotted the the 1976 Games in Montreal after the IOC refused to ban New Zealand from the Games.

- New Zealand's rugby team (the All Blacks) had toured South Africa, a country that had been banned from the Olympics since 1964 because of its APARTHEID policies (segregation based on ethnicity/colour).

- As a result of the terrorism in Munich, the security costs ended up running to another $100 million (more than 80% of what initial costs for the whole event were supposed to be!)

- These events contributed to $1.6 billion debt for the city, eventually paid off in 2006...

DEVELOPMENTS IN THE MEDIA

NEWSPAPERS

- The first real source of media came from the newspapers.
- This was expanded quickly with the emergence of sports journalism.
- There was the introduction of a sports column & sports pages as well as papers dedicated to sport. eg The Bell's life & Sporting Chronicle were weekly papers published every Saturday between 1822-1886.
- By the 1920s sports reports were popular & had mass appeal to a wide ranging audience.
- Today, many 'pundits' cover a wide range of sports with greater analysis.
- In 1911 the 'Football Players' Magazine - Official Journal of the Association Football Players Union, was launched by Evelyn Lintott. This led the way for many sports publications seen today.

DEVELOPMENTS

- Media outlets & sources increased in popularity due to the rise in SPECTATORISM.
- The media liked to promote their local sporting heroes & businesses started to use the media, to promote their goods & services.

RADIO

- Radio commentary got off to a rocky start as the Newspaper Proprietors Association argued that radio was a rival form of news reporting & was able to block attempts at commentary by the British Broadcasting Company (BBC).
- In 1923 the Parliamentary Sykes Committee on broadcasting was concerned that any broadcasting of sports results would harm newspaper sales, but felt it might be acceptable to cover some 'special' outside events.
- The rules were relaxed a few years later & the BBC introduced sports commentary in 1927 when Teddy Wakelam covered England v Wales (rugby). Wakelam then covered football & tennis from Wimbledon.
- Commentary on radio still continues today (5 Live), but has been overshadowed by visual technology (TV).
- Today sport can be covered online, on TV, satellite TV, via computer & mobiles.

TELEVISION

- The Epsom Derby was the first televised sporting event covered in Britain in 1931.
- The Wimbledon Tennis Championship was televised for the first time in June 1937, with Fred Perry the reigning champion.
- The first televised football match was 16th September 1937 between Arsenal & Arsenal reserves.
- Development of TV slowed down for the masses after WWII, though expanded quickly in the 1950s.

FRANCHISES IN SPORT

A FRANCHISE

- ... is where any person(s) buy the contractual rights to buy a team to operate this team in a specific location in any competition.

- Franchises are very much how the USA professional sports system works in major competitions, such as the NBA, NFL, NHL, MLB & MLS.

- Other countries such as Australia & New Zealand not also adopt a similar approach that is in contrast to the blue European system.

- They are obviously private investors with the view of not just creating a successful sporting team, but to make a profit (often the drive for profit is more important than sporting success).
  eg as part of his MLS contract with LA Galaxy, David Beckham was allowed to buy a discounted "franchise to be based in Miami".

THE PROS

- There are less salary restrictions. Money from various avenues/streams can be used to secure players.
- No relegation, reducing the negative (& often toxic) manager sackings & financial loss.
- More teams have a realistic chance to win the championship.
- Stadia & spectator facilities are excellent due to private (& local government) investment & the pride taken to create an entertaining environment.
- Increase in higher entertainment & level / even games with a play-off system.
- Draft system with the previous years teams who did not perform well gaining higher draft picks to try and 'even things out.'
- Due to no relegation, the best players play in the competition all the time (not as many weak teams coming up from the leagues below).

THE CONS

- Differences in ticket prices with different parts of the country paying more/less. eg costs more to watch basketball in New York at Madison Square Garden than the equivalent game at the Amway Centre in Orlando.
- Communities can lose their teams as the franchise moves markets. eg 2008 Seattle Supersonics relocated & rebranded as Oklahoma Thunder in Oklahoma City. Why? Local government refused $500 million stadia investment.
- New teams cannot enter the league unless the league board members decide/agree to expand the competition (as recently with the MLS).
- Teams that do not make the play-offs have shorter seasons.
- Boring! Little variety.

102

THE GOLDEN TRIANGLE

- Has allowed elite sports to develop down the lines of an **AMERICANISATION model.**

- This is where the influence of American culture & business has provided sport with not only a means of entertainment, but also as a business with the sale of TV rights, becoming a major source of sports funding.

- This has helped sports increase in popularity globally, with major sporting events that have traditionally only been played in their home country, having games played overseas. eg **USA, NFL & MLB** games played in London and the opening stage of the Tour de France regularly starting in Spain, Belgium, Holland & England.

LINKAGE

- ... is key! Shows **how money can be made** by sporting events eg the **Olympic Games** - Sponsors (The Olympic Partner Programme) - **Media** - NBC.

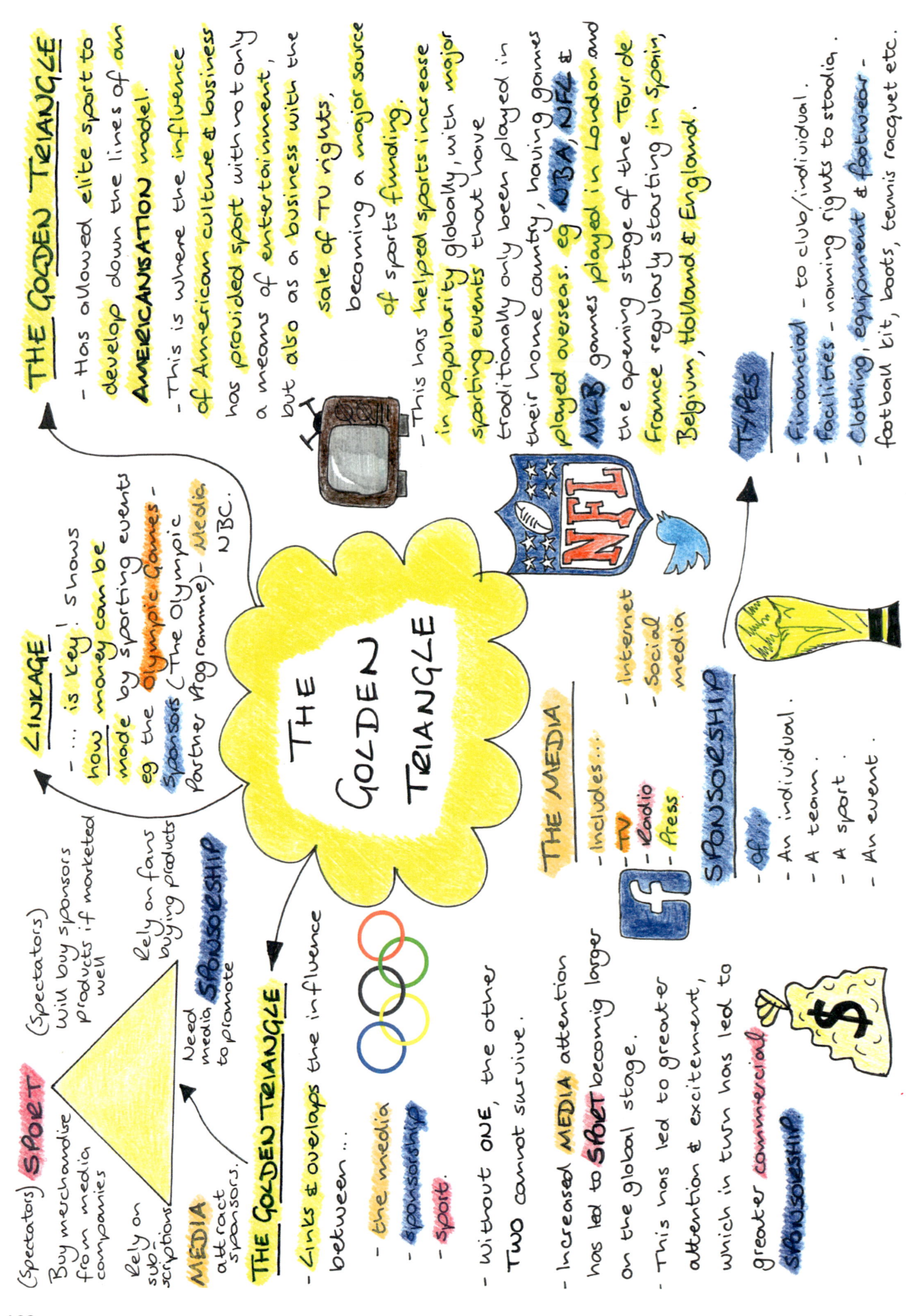

THE GOLDEN TRIANGLE

- Links & overlaps the influence between...
  - the media
  - sponsorship
  - sport.

- Without ONE, the other TWO cannot survive.

- Increased **MEDIA** attention has led to **SPORT** becoming larger on the global stage.
- This has led to greater attention & excitement, which in turn has led to greater **commercial SPONSORSHIP**

THE GOLDEN TRIANGLE

(Spectators) **SPORT**
(Spectators) Buy merchandise from media companies
Rely on subscriptions

MEDIA attract sponsors.

Will buy sponsors products if marketed well

Rely on fans buying products

Need media & **SPONSORSHIP** to promote

THE MEDIA
- Includes...
  - TV
  - Radio
  - Press
  - Internet
  - Social media

SPONSORSHIP
- of:
  - An individual.
  - A team.
  - A sport.
  - An event.

TYPES
- Financial - to club/individual.
- Facilities - naming rights to stadia.
- Clothing, equipment & footwear - football kit, boots, tennis racquet etc.

103

Pros & Cons of the Golden Triangle

- As with everything, there are **BENEFITS & DRAWBACKS** associated with the **GOLDEN TRIANGLE**, but remember, there are **3** sides to consider... (as it is a triangle!)

CONS

- If the team performs badly, funding may be withdrawn, or a major sponsor could leave, putting the club/franchise under financial strain.

- Only high profile sports & performers attract media attention & sponsorship (especially during prime-time slots). Minority sports & their players miss out.
  eg table tennis.

- The influence of investors & sponsors has taken away some power from NGBs. eg TV time outs, the 7th innings stretch in baseball for commercials.

- Sponsors restrictions for some performers, depending on the team they play for. May be a Nike v Adidas clash!

- Increased pressure to succeed has led to an increase in deviant behaviour.

- Media intrusion on decision making with action replays & VAR/TMO etc.

- Kick off times, dates changed to suit media requirements, not fans!

- An increase in ticket prices as players' wages increase.

PROS

- An increase in global & diverse role models & global superstars.
  eg Michael Jordan put basketball & the Chicago Bulls on the global stage during the late 1980s & 1990s. (See the 'Last Dance' on Netflix).

- David Beckham became a global star & helped Manchester United become the next 'big franchise' after the Chicago Bulls era.

- Today Lionel Messi, LeBron James, Cristiano Ronaldo, Kylian Mbappe, Serena Williams

- Greater levels of sponsorship have increased player & coach wages, in turn improving playing standards.

- Popularity of sport increases due to an increase in media coverage/exposure.

- Profits made can be reinvested into developing the sport at grassroots level & to improve facilities (but are they?)

- New formats & rules evolve to attract a wider audience.
  eg Twenty 20 cricket. The 100 cricket.

ETHICS & DEVIANCE IN SPORT

REASONS FOR DEVIANT BEHAVIOUR

- 'Win at all costs' mentality.
- Team or sport culture. eg to win the Tour de France some think you need to take PEDs in order to level the playing field (as everyone else uses them).
- Pressure to win (from coach, sponsors).
- To secure a new contract.
- Pressure from leader in a team. eg Cycling & Lance Armstrong.
- Media/social media pressure.
- Lack of moral compass. Why not?
- Copy deviant role models. eg Tyson Gay, Ben Johnson in athletics.
- Reacting to frustration or actions of opponents eg sledging in cricket can lead to aggressive acts.
- To gain 'an edge' physically and/or psychologically.
- Stress of competition.

EXAMPLES

Include...
- Violence & hostile aggression
- Taking PEDs
- Match fixing / betting
- Diving ... or is that Gamesmanship?

ETHICS

- Refers to unwritten rules concerning player behaviour (etiquette), referring to the spirit of the game in sport.
- eg kicking the ball out of play if an opponent is injured (genuinely!) in football.

DEVIANCE

- Is unacceptable behaviour that differs from the perceived social & legal norm which is usually against the laws of the activity & as such is viewed as unethical. Put simply, it is cheating; breaking the rule in an illegal manner.
- It can be the result of the desire & drive to 'win at all costs'
- eg taking Performance Enhancing Drugs (PEDs) in order to win at an athletic event.

CONSEQUENCES OF DEVIANT BEHAVIOUR

- Reputation damage to the sport. eg cycling, athletics.
- Reputation damage to the country. eg Russia (banned!)
- Punishments. eg bans, fines, suspensions, medals taken away.
- Lack of trust - fans, sponsors.
- Loss of earnings (past & future).
- Negative role model status; respect lost!

SPORTSMANSHIP AND GAMESMANSHIP

COMMERCIALISM

- The increase in commercialism has had many positive effects on sport.
- ... however due to increased pressure on performance & a 'win at all costs' attitude at the elite level, the rise in issues surrounding gamesmanship has increased.
- Players vie for bigger deals (both in terms of contracts with their team and sponsorship deals).
- The pressure to secure their legacy & future prospects can come down to a single game or event.
- At times there is not always a clear line between gamesmanship & deviant behaviour (eg diving/ simulation in football).
- This is one of the reasons why the increase in technology on the court/pitch has helped to eradicate certain behaviours (eg off the ball incidents in football that may be missed by the referee).
- Such technology includes... replays, pitch side microphones & numerous camera angles.

ETIQUETTE

- Is the way sportsmen/women behave whilst playing (in a positive manner). Very similar to sportsmanship. Promotes fair play

SPORTSMANSHIP

- Play & abide by the rules, win & lose graciously. Sportsmen & women are role models & should adhere to the written (& unwritten!) rules of the sport.
- Fair play, respect & polite behaviours are all important. eg shaking hands at the end of the game. Helping an injured opponent. Being respectful to officials.

GAMESMANSHIP

- 'The use of dubious though not illegal methods to win or gain an advantage.'
  'Bending' the rules not breaking them!
- All done with the intention of winning!
  eg timewasting in football, sledging in cricket to get a psychological advantage & diving in football after a tackle to influence the ref to give a free kick ... or is it DEVIANCE!?

CONTRACT TO COMPETE

- agreeing to play by the rules, trying to win, but also allowing your opponent to play.
- Want to win, but not at all costs!
- Links with etiquette & sportsmanship.

EXAMPLES OF PED USE

- Include:
  - Racehorses in the 1900s given substances to increase their speed.

- The Soviet & East German state-funded doping regime post WWII was at its height during the 1970's & 80's. Idea to show the success of the Communist state.

- In 1988, one of the biggest drug-taking scandals occurred at the Seoul Olympics, with the winner of the 100m mens final, (Ben Johnson of Canada) testing positive for Stanozolol – an Anabolic Agent/steroid.

- Tyson Gay (2012) failed 3 drug tests in quick succession and as a result lost the medals he had won at the London 2012 Games.

* There are many, many more examples than the ones listed here.

DEVIANCE in sport can take many forms, including...
- Performance Enhancing Drugs
- Blood Doping & Transfusions
- Simulation (diving)
- Bribery
- Bungs
- Match fixing
- Betting Syndicates

SPORT AND DEVIANCE

- After an investigation, it was concluded that Russia ran a state sponsored doping programme from 2011 & have been banned from all major international events since 2016.

- cleared individual athletes have been allowed to compete under the IOC flag.

PERFORMANCE ENHANCING DRUGS

PEDs for short.

- Includes...
- STIMULANTS
- NARCOTIC ANALGESICS
- BETA BLOCKERS
- ANABOLIC AGENTS
- PEPTIDE HORMONES
- DIURETICS

- Drug use to enhance performance has been a problem in sport for a long time.

- Some researchers state that PEDs were used in Ancient Greek times, with athletes using hallucinogenic mushrooms, sesame seeds and brandy/wine mixtures to enhance performance.

- In the current climate, PEDs have become a lucrative source of income on the black market.

- The temptation for some athletes to secure victory & their legacy has been too much.

- As the technology surrounding PEDs ever increases, so too does the technology for testing to catch drug cheats. More on this on page 111.

107

Sport And Deviance

Diuretics

- Are 'masking agents' taken to flush out other drugs.
- Aid weight loss as they speed up urine production & so lose excess fluids.

Benefits - aid performers that need to make a weight category eg jockey, boxer, wrestler, sumo.

Side Effects - dehydration, kidney damage, nausea, headaches.

Narcotic Analgesics

- Painkillers. Can mask injury from impact or overtraining.
- Can though make it worse eg muscle tears.
- Allows the performer to compete when injured. eg Morphine, Cortisone.

Benefits - will aid any injured performer.

Side Effects - highly addictive, can cause more damage to the injury, lack of focus, anxiety & depression.

* As with all PEDs, the side effects, both short & long term far outweigh any potential benefits.
∴ death (potentially!)

Blood Doping & Transfusions

- Blood doping is not the use of PEDs. It is a process.
- Although 'doping' is a generic term used to label taking PEDs, blood doping refers to the injection of oxygen rich blood into an athlete in an illegal attempt to boost/enhance performance (mainly used in long distance endurance events eg cycling).
- Can give a 20% improvement in carrying O₂ to working muscles.
- In 2012, one of the biggest/most famous doping scandals was that of Lance Armstrong (7 time Tour de France winner).
- After mounting pressure, he admitted to blood doping (to enhance performance) & was later stripped of his titles.
- PEDs are still prevalent (sadly) in cycling & according to surveys an estimated 90% of cyclists have admitted to drug use!

- Max Hauke, an Austrian cross-country skier was arrested in 2019 after evidence was found on video of him carrying out a blood transfusion.
- He admitted to this and also taking a Human Growth Hormone & was jailed for 5 months & banned for 4 years until 2023.

SPORT AND DEVIANCE

MATCH FIXING

- Occurs when a game or match is influenced (generally for financial gain).
- eg in the London 2012 Olympic Games, the Chinese, Indonesian & South Korean badminton teams were found to be losing deliberately in order to face potentially 'easier' teams in the latter stages. All teams were disqualified & charged with abusing & demeaning the sport of badminton.

A BUNG

- Is an unauthorised & undisclosed payment to a person (in a high position) at a club.
- Agents attempting to get the best deal for their player may pay the manager 'a bung'.

SIMULATION

- ... aka diving!
- Is an unsportsmanlike act whereby a player tries to gain an unfair advantage by pretending to have been fouled & falling to the ground, with the aim of influencing the referee to give a foul, waste time, or get the opposition player booked.
- In 2017/18 the FA updated the rule on simulation & diving & have stated it must be sanctioned as unsporting behaviour (misconduct, punishable by a yellow card).
- Instances of simulation can also now be looked at retrospectively, if missed by the referee.

BETTING SYNDICATES

- Are a type of pool betting, involving two or more people that predict results of sporting events & provide odds for gamblers.
- eg in 2010, young Pakistani fast bowler Mohammed Amir was found guilty of bowling deliberate illegal deliveries (no balls) in a test series v England, in order to fall in with bets placed by syndicates. This got Amir banned from Pakistani Cricket for 5 yrs, alongside fellow pace bowler Mohammed Asif & captain Salman Butt for the same length of time by the ICC.

BRIBERY

- A bribe is where someone takes/receives something with the intention of influencing the outcome.
- eg Sepp Blatter (former FIFA president) was found to have accepted undue economic benefits (£18 million or so) for various conflicts of interest in relation to awarding various tournaments to various countries dating back to 2011.
- This included the world Cups to Russia (2018) & Qatar (2022).
- Blatter was banned from any involvement in football for 6 years (from 2015). In 2021 he was given another 6 years & 8 months suspension.

COMBATTING DEVIANT BEHAVIOUR

SPORT & THE LAW

- Have traditionally been considered as separate areas.

- However more recently there have been an increasing amount of lawsuits due to deviant acts or breaches of contract.

Sport & the Law (Rugby)

- eg Australian rugby players Israel Folau had his contract terminated with Rugby Australia in 2019 for a post on social media regarding homosexuality & his faith.

- However Folau took legal action & an out of court settlement was agreed.

Sport & the Law (Football)

- Issues relating to violent acts are mostly dealt with by clubs or the NGB's as they have their own judicial system, but sometimes violent or unlawful acts in sport can be prosecuted outside of sport.

- eg 18 yr old Ben Collett was playing for Manchester United v Middlesborough in 2008, when he was tackled by Gary Smith; a tackle that was high & over the ball. As a result Collett fractured his tibia & fibula of his right leg.

- Collett pursued the club (Middlesborough), not Smith, arguing that they were liable for their employees actions, given he was connected to the club & acting in his employment as a professional footballer.

- Middlesborough admitted liability & Collett awarded £4.3 million damages.

NGB's

- Are responsible for creating the rules & regulations that govern their sport.

- These are based on a set of principles, policies, products that provide safety in equipment & facilities and that support the moral values of fair play & sportsmanship.

IGB's

- Of a particular sport will be the regulator, developing the laws of the game for that sport.

- These will then be expected to be regulated by various member countries own NGB's.

ELITE SPORT

- Has become more commercialised & exposed in the media, so any inappropriate behaviours is more likely to attract the attention of law enforcing agencies. Sport is seen by the law as a 'special area' where by the law & legal systems do not directly interfere with the specific rules in relation to that specific sport.

Elite Sport (Bosman)

- Performers/players are employees - they have a contract & employment rights.

- In 1995 THE BOSMAN RULING meant that players could move to a new club at the end of their contract without a fee being paid. Can now sign pre-contract agreements if their current deal has less than 1/2 months remaining.

HUNT DOWN

The drug cheats. Test...

HAIR
URINE
NAILS
TEST BLOOD

DRUG TESTING

- First occurred in 1966 European Athletic championships in Budapest, then 2 years later at the 1968 Olympics in Mexico City.

- A sample tests positive, test B sample. B sample positive = BAN. 1st offence = 4 years.

BIOLOGICAL PASSPORT

- Since 2009, WADA first approved its use, it has been an effective deterrent & way of catching drug cheats.

- Anti-doping organisations have integrated the Biological Passport into their programme to reveal the effects of doping rather than the method or substance used.

- The first version profiled an Athletes haematological variables (for the detection of blood doping). In 2014 the steroidal Module was launched to complement this, focussing on an athlete's steroid variables in urine samples.

- ...however this new data has given athletes insight into doping techniques. Further advanced techniques have been developed regards 'microdosing' or sequential smaller doses of EPO. Just enough of a boost, but too small to spike/dip the data!

THE WORLD ANTI-DOPING AGENCY - WADA

THE ROLE OF WADA

- Founded in 1999, an International Independent Agency, funded by the sports movement & national governments.

- WADA aims to bring consistency to anti-doping policies & regulations within sports organisations & governments worldwide. Leads a collaborative worldwide movement for 'doping free' sport

- Plays the lead role in scientific, research, education & developing anti-doping capabilities & monitoring.

(World Anti-Doping Code).

- Governments, IGBs & NGBs agree to this code & 'sign up' as signatories.

- Within WADA there is an intelligence & investigation team that work with law enforcement to target & shut down large scale doping rings.

WHEREABOUTS RULE

- Introduced in 2004.

- Athletes must provide details of their location for one hour everyday between 5am & 11pm, to their Anti-Doping Agency (eg UK Anti-Doping)

- 2015 - standard 2 year ban for missing 3 in 12 months.

- eg 2003 Rio Ferdinand was banned for 8 months & fined £50,000 for failing to take a test.

Combatting Deviant Behaviour

THE COURT OF ARBITRATION FOR SPORT (CAS)

- Is often referred to as... 'sport's Supreme Court'.
- An institution independent of any sports organisation that provides a service to facilitate the settlement of sport related disputes (directly or indirectly linked to sport may be submitted to CAS).
- These may be disputes of a commercial nature (a sponsorship deal) or of a disciplinary nature following a decision by a sports organisation (ban for doping).

SEGREGATION OF FANS
- keep opposing fans apart. Gap with stewards/police. (Again costly).

Referees/officials/coaches have
- a duty of care to protect participants in competition.
- Negligence cases have been brought against referees. eg collapsed scrum injuring players, concussion management in 1990s-2000s by the IRB.

IMPROVED SECURITY
- checks at turnstiles, CCTV inside & out, more police, better trained stewards, police spotters. (Costly).

FAMILY FRIENDLY
- as a result less instances of violence.

EDUCATIONAL CAMPAIGNS
- Players/role models used. eg 'Kick it Out'.

SUPPORTERS

- Legal action against supporters does occur, with some forms of unacceptable behaviour becoming more commonplace (eg attacking players, officials, running onto the pitch).

- Spectators must act within the law when at a game.

- They are not permitted to enter the field of play or use racist/homophobic language, something most NGBs are trying to eradicate with the help of 'Kick it Out'.

GOOD spectator behaviour or etiquette means watching & behaving in a respectful manner.
eg not booing the opposing national anthem, being quiet during rallies in tennis, place kicks in rugby & tee shots in golf.

- Clubs & sports governing bodies employ a number of strategies focussed on spectator behaviour, including

ALCOHOL RESTRICTIONS & KICK OFFS
- Games start before the pubs open. Limit sales, banned in the away end (though this may cause trouble?). Not allowed in view of the pitch (football)

TRAVEL RESTRICTIONS & BANNING ORDERS
- stop known hooligans attending games. Attend police station on match day. Bans, fines...even prison!

THE IMPACT OF TECHNOLOGY IN

HAWKEYE

- Has been revolutionary in both tennis & cricket, where the software follows the trajectory of the ball, allowing for action replays for the fans in the stadium/ground, or the armchair fan at home. eg used when players challenge decisions if given out in cricket, or the ball is called out in tennis.

- Now also used for goal line technology (to see if the ball crossed the goal line). Linked to referee.

TIMING GATES

- Used in alpine skiing so skiers can track their pace throughout each stage of a race. Allows the viewers at home to do the same.

GLOBAL POSITIONING SYSTEM - GPS

- At times GPS data has been shared by broadcasters showing heart rates, metres covered & top speed to viewers in some rugby matches.

SLOW MOTION CAMERAS

- High definition (HD) cameras are used as photo finish devices in a 100m sprint race, allowing viewers to get a realistic look at the finish.

ON THE VIEWING EXPERIENCE

- Technological advancements on how sport is brought to the armchair fan at home is continually improving, bringing the audience close to the action in an almost virtual sense.

SPIDERCAM

- Has been used to show a 'bird's eye' view looking down onto the playing surface.

- Allows viewers to gain an insight into different formations, plays, running lines & fielding positions from another perspective. eg Spidercam hovering over a football pitch looking downwards to show player movements & formations.

CAMERAS/MINI-CAMERAS

- Used in many sports & by many officials. Referees use them as part of the review process (VAR). Cameras underwater are used to help adjudicate positions in swimming & the viewers can also follow a performer competing in a BMX race from a helmet-cam. eg GoPro.

INCLUDES

113

SPORT AND THE MEDIA

TIMELINE

1937 – First major sport event broadcast live. Wimbledon with Bunny Austin v George Rogers on the BBC.

1948 – The London Olympics was broadcast to viewers in London only.

1966 – The World Cup final (England v W. Germany) was televised in colour to an audience of 32.3 million.

1975 – 'The Thriller in Manila' Mohammed Ali v Joe Frazier was the first action to be broadcast from overseas via satellite.

1990 – Sky covers England v West Indies from Jamaica.

1991 – Sky TV launches Sky Sports.

1996 – First UK pay per view event. Frank Bruno v Mike Tyson, broadcast on Sky.

2006 – The World Cup in Germany was the first sports event broadcast in HD (high definition) on BBC. 5 of the games most watched programmes in 2006.

2010 – Sky launches the UK's first 3D channel.

2011 – Sky Go launched for mobile devices (eg phone). Watch Sky channels 'on the go'.

2012 – London 2012, an estimated global audience 1bn watched the opening ceremony. The BBC showed more than 2,500 hrs of live sport + 3D.

SPORT & THE MEDIA

- ... now appear to have a very symbiotic relationship.

- Throw in sponsorship and you have the golden triangle

REASONS FOR THE GROWTH OF LIVE/SOCIAL MEDIA

- The globalisation of sport has led to extensive media coverage. eg Euro 2020 on both BBC & ITV. Fan bases for major sports & performers reach for & wide around the world (impact of gaming also?)

- Sports & performers have become commodities with regard to commercialisation.

- This economic value has led to the rise in satellite events & social media.

- Sponsors associated with sport use various media platforms to advertise their company...

SPORTS JOURNALISM

- Started to develop in the 1800s (see page 84) & the introduction of sports columns like Bell's Life (1822) & Sports Life (1860s) promoted sport & sporting icons.

- More appealing specialist papers dedicated to sport (especially football & rugby) were introduced in the 1920s.

- Today, popular tabloids like the Mirror & Daily Mail, plus the Guardian (broadsheet) are available online (as are most newspapers).

- The development of television gradually increased throughout the 20th century & beyond. A (brief) major timeline is listed to the right.

114

SPORTS MEDIA PACKAGES

ADVANTAGES

- Huge amount of choice with the different broadcasters.

- Can pay either as a one-off or a monthly subscription.

- There is not just PPV, but iPPV, where live global streaming ensures that big events can be watched at home or on the go.

- Big events & popular matches can be viewed as terrestrial TV (BBC, ITV, CH5, CH4) do not usually show them (cost in bidding rights).

- Some big clubs like Manchester United have their own channel; MUTV. May get subscription included if you are a club member, if not it is extra.

- Sponsors can recognise the value in PPV or subscription based events. They pick & target certain events eg Lions Tour to advertise hoping to increase their economic value & reach of their company/products.

DISADVANTAGES

- Can be very, very expensive if want to watch a range of sports via different broadcasters.

- Installation of specialist equipment can be expensive & time-consuming.

- Armchair fans can affect the numbers at live venues, having a negative impact on revenue.

- Fibre-optic broadband (for high quality streaming) not available everywhere.

- Packages usually focus on popular sports (football, rugby) so minority sports miss out.

PACKAGES

- BT Sports, Sky Sports & Virgin Media are just a few of the main media outlets that offer a wide range of sports packages that can be specifically designed to meet the needs of the viewers.

Virgin media

- The number of sports channels is ever increasing, with more sports getting their own Sky Sports channel, including...
  - Football
  - Cricket
  - Formula 1
  - Golf

Sky even has it's own Sky Sports News channel.

- Pay per view (PPV) is a system where viewers pay a fee for special programmes (Live Events or sports). Mainly used for Boxing & UFC.

- The biggest PPV in history was Floyd Mayweather Jr v Connor McGregor in 2017, with 6.7 million buys & total revenue of $700m for a 'sham' fight!

TALENT IDENTIFICATION

IN EAST GERMANY

- After WWII Germany was split in 2...

EAST GERMANY was controlled by the Soviets, & WEST GERMANY, controlled (initially) by Britain, the USA & France.

- The results were analysed & those that scored highly on the biometric & sporting/fitness tests were invited to attend local training centres several times per week.

East Germany / West Germany

EAST GERMANY

East Germany pioneered the CENTRALISED MODEL of talent ID & routes to the elite level.

- As mentioned above, it was a newly created country after WWII & they decided to use sport (especially the Olympics) as a SHOP WINDOW to showcase their success & gain recognition internationally.

- The talent ID programme was state sponsored & began in Primary Schools, where 7 years old children were screened for sporting potential.

- If the students met the elite criteria by the age of 10½, they were sent to sports boarding schools.

- Here, the main emphasis was on sports development. Students trained 6 hours per day, with just 2 hours of academic study, 6 days a week!

- Annual SPARTAKIAD events were held, with elite athletes competing against one another.

These were funded by the (then) Soviet Union.

- When students graduated from the sports boarding schools, athletes could then base themselves at one of eight national centres full time, with access to high quality facilities, coaching & sports science.

- Although the programme was funded, it was the state doping programme that operated 'hand in hand' with the talent ID & coaching that led to it's downfall.

East German National Squad ↑
National Sports Institute ↑
State run sports club ↑
Annual Spartakiad ↑
Sports boarding school ↑
Primary school talent ID programme

TALENT IDENTIFICATION

IN AUSTRALIA

- Similar to the East German model, Australia adopted a more centralised approach to talent ID after the unsuccessful & national embarrassing performance in the Montreal Olympics in 1976.
- Australia performed poorly, winning only one silver & four bronze medals, finishing 32nd in the medals table.
- What was even worse, was the fact they lost to their neighbours New Zealand 1-0 in the Men's hockey final.
- As a result of this, the Australian government undertook a review of its elite sports system, favouring a centralised system/model, with the AUSTRALIAN INSTITUTE of SPORT (AIS) opening just outside the capital, Canberra, in 1981.
- The AIS at the time was the envy of the world & now offers multiple scholarships in a wide variety of sports.

- The centre offers top class coaching & sports science support and branches out into all states in Australia (7), with their own satellite institutions in all state capitals.
- Similar to the East German model, the (Australian) AIS developed a Sports Search talent ID programme, where children around Australia performed a range of fitness tests during PE lessons. Results were recorded & based on results, details of local clubs were advertised that suited the individual children.
- More exceptional children were invited to Sports Institutes for further screening.
- The programme was very elitist, only taking the top athletes.
- However over a 24 year period Australia went from 32nd place in the 1976 Olympics to 4th in their home Sydney Olympics in 2000.
- Below is the talent ID model for South Australia, similar to the one used in most states.

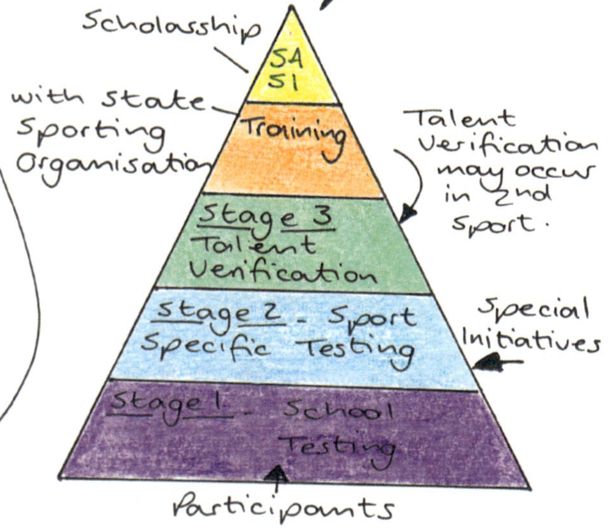
Scholarship
SA
SI
with state Sporting Organisation
Training
Stage 3 Talent Verification
Talent Verification may occur in 2nd sport.
Stage 2 - Sport Specific Testing
Special Initiatives
Stage 1 - School Testing
Participants

TALENT IDENTIFICATION

UK SPORT TALENT ID MODEL
- Multiple phases when looking for talent.
- Campaigns start with a local talent search, either with the general public or with the sports communities involving athletes submitting an application form to UK sport.

AND DEVELOPMENT IN THE UK
- The GB team & UK Sport went through hard times in the 1990s, but an announcement on the 1st March 1999 by the Government expanding the UK sports institutes (UKSI) provision, with a view to concentrating on Olympic sports & those minority sports lacking a commercial element.
- Similar to the Australian model, the UKSI is supported by a network of centres across England... Bath University, Milton Keynes, Bisham Abbey, Crystal Palace, Gateshead, Holme Pierrepont/Loughborough, Lilleshall, Manchester, Southampton University & Sheffield (where the EIS is located).
- Home nations also have national centres in...
  Scotland
  Wales
  Northern Ireland.

UK SPORT
- They analyse the applications & successful athletes/people are invited to start the phase process outlined below...

PHASE ONE
- A range of generic physical & skill based tests (carried out at various testing centres around the UK).
- Tests include... sprints, jumps, aerobic fitness & upper/lower body strength tests.
- Specific tests will depend on the sport.
- Selection process also includes an in depth analysis of each athlete's training & competition history.

CONFIRMATION PHASE
- Athletes selected need to commit to 6-12 months confirmation phase.
- Immersed into the sports training environment.
- Rates of progress are tracked to further assess suitability.
- Unsuccessful athletes move towards club system.

PHASE TWO & THREE
- Are designed to further assess an athlete's suitability for a sport & better equip them for the journey ahead.
- The pathway from identification to world class performance is outlined.
- Sessions may include... functional movement screening, medical screening, performance lifestyle workshops & psychology and behavioural assessments.

TALENT ID INITIATIVES

WORLD CLASS PROGRAMME

- Funded & run by UK Sport (the elite sports agency in the UK).

WORLD CLASS PODIUM

- Designed to support sports & athletes with medal capabilities (realistic) at Olympic Games or gold medal capabilities (realistic) at Paralympic Games.

- Are a maximum of 4 years away from the podium.

WORLD CLASS PODIUM POTENTIAL

- Designed to support the stage of the pathway immediately below podium.

- Supports sports & athletes that have demonstrated realistic medal winning capabilities for future Olympic or Paralympic Games.

- Typically 4-6 years away from the podium.

PERFORMANCE FOUNDATIONS

- Home Nations Talent Pathways where highly talented athletes are first identified, confirmed & prepared to meet the increased demands of the World Class environment.

- Athletes at PF level have the potential to graduate to PP within 1-4 years.

(list of levels:)
- Podium
- Podium Potential
- Performance Foundations
- National Age Group Progs
- Regional Programmes
- County Programmes
- Community School etc.

CURRENTLY

- UK Sport & the EIS work together with Team GB & Paralympics GB in search of athletes of the future called

FROM HOME 2 THE GAMES.

- The initiative has been designed to discover untapped potential from all communities in the UK.

- More specifically 11-23 year olds who are physically active to participate in an Olympic sport & 15-34 year olds with an impairment that makes them eligible in a Paralympic sport.

- Different initiatives are conducted at different points, but specific eg's include...

BOUNCE 4 GOLD - 12-15 year old gymnasts

POWER 2 PARIS - Paralympic cyclists.

TALENT ID IN THE PRIVATE SECTOR

- Football & rugby (where there is ample commercial investment) tend to have a slightly different model.

- Individual clubs have their own scouting network where they aim to recruit young players with the right qualities (in terms of technical ability, physicality & mental skills) into their academies.

- Success in the academies will lead to professional status either with their club or further afield.

- However, in the case of football, less than 0.5% of academy players ever make the top level!

MASS PARTICIPATION

MASS PARTICIPATION

- The concept of mass participation refers to encouraging as many people as possible to participate in some form of physical activity, or to take up an active lifestyle.

- There are many benefits to this, including...

- Healthier nation & less strain on the NHS.
- Less money spent on hypokinetic diseases eg diabetes.
- Build social networks in communities.
- Reduce crime, safer neighbourhoods.
- Improve educational standards.
- Improve confidence & promote positive behaviours.
- Widens base of participation pyramid, possibly leading to greater success at elite level.

BARRIERS TO PARTICIPATION

- Certain factors do not allow for mass participation.
- Think of GLASED

  - GENDER
  - LOCATION
  - AGE
  - Socio-Economic
  - ETHNICITY
  - DISABILITY

GENDER

- Most sports played by both sexes now eg football, rugby. Netball still less media coverage.
- #ThisGirlCan campaign launched in 2015 hugely successful.
- Activity Rates - 65% men * 61% women *
- * Active Lives survey 2018-19. regularly participate in sport.
- Why? - traditional roles (homemaker), less role models.

LOCATION

- Ability to access facilities/ resources.
- Locality a huge factor. Near a pool or leisure centre?
- Can you access transport to/from?
- Near the outdoors? eg The Lakes.

AGE

- Age restrictions on some sports. eg Boxing.
- As you get older, more responsibilities (work, children), less 'leisure time'.
- OAP's - stereotype of playing bowls & golf. Social side of sport very important.
- Children - rely on parents for transport & to pay for clubs (links to socio-economic).

Socio-Economic

- Focus on cost & disposable income.'
- Equipment, clothing & membership can be very expensive. eg golf, cricket.
- Too expensive for some eg unemployed, working class.

ETHNICITY

- Religion & culture can influence sports played. eg cricket.
- Racist abuse still aimed at Black footballers, as seen in recent football matches. (Euro 2020).

DISABILITY

- Or ability.
- Now a much higher profile after London 2012 (at elite level).
- Barriers still at local/school level. Issues = funding, access, equipment, discrimination & accessible sessions.

INITIATIVES

- Both YST & SPORT ENGLAND are actively involved in funding & introducing programmes that encourage participation & target the population & target groups.

ACTIVE ACROSS AGES

- Developed as a pilot project to improve the physical, mental & social wellbeing of participants, provide volunteering opportunities, develop employability skills/confidence & to be physically active.
- Also provides opportunities to support primary to secondary transition & enhance local community relationships between young people & older adults.

SAINSBURY'S ACTIVE KIDS FOR ALL INCLUSIVE PE TRAINING

- Provides training & resources to support teachers, trainees & school staff to provide high quality PE lessons for children.

The YOUTH SPORT TRUST along with SPORT ENGLAND implement numerous initiatives & programmes that target certain groups who may be unable to access sport and/or physical activity, including...

BREAKING BOUNDARIES

- Aim - to socially connect young people, families & communities together through regular cricket engagement.
- Delivered in 5 cities... Bradford, Birmingham, Manchester, Slough & London.

GIRLS ACTIVE

- Aim - to improve girls/attitudes towards PE, increase participation in PE & sport, improve self-esteem & confidence and to improve school-student relationships in PE & across the school.

BOYS MOVE

- An approach that addresses the wellbeing challenges of working class boys through PE & sport.

BEE WELL

- To be rolled out across secondary schools in Greater Manchester for 3 years (Autumn 2021). Aim to improve wellbeing of young people.

SCHOOL GAMES

- Funded by Sport England, delivered by YST, the School Games started in 2006 as a single annual multi-sport competition, with a National Final.
- In 2010, it was expanded to include more localised competitions, with major county events to smaller competitions within the same school.

WEARABLE TECHNOLOGY

BENEFITS

- Provides people with the ability to track & monitor fitness levels, location & movement intensity with **GPS**.
- Most of the devices are hands-free & portable.
- 'Wearables' are connected to smart devices, transmitting this information to them to view in real time &/or later.
- Can help people set goals & take more responsibility in tracking health & progress (rather than relying on someone else).

DRAWBACKS

- Short battery life; some functions may not work to save battery life. eg Apple watches have a shorter battery life than a fit-bit tracker.
- Reports of inaccurate data being measured & inconsistencies between different devices/apps (eg Strava & Nike Run club). Could be dangerous if tracking HR for a heart condition.
- No conclusive evidence that the rise has increased participation rates.
- Cost ££$¢

WEARABLE TECH

As with most things, there are **Pros & Cons** associated with wearable technology. Most tech is very expensive & once you rely on the data it produces, it is hard to do without.

- Has become increasingly popular in recent years & has been available since the mid 2000s.
- Aim ... to provide innovative ways to address physical inactivity issues & increasing sedentary lifestyles that have become part & parcel of modern day life (sadly!)
- Wearable technology such as...
  - smartphones
  - smart watches
  - wristbands
  - GPS devices

  are self-tracking tools that are capable of monitoring heart rate, weight, intensity levels, movement patterns, sleep, diet & emotions.
- According to a survey by Atest in 2019, 37.6% of 'millenials' own a smart watch with a health tracker.
- Statista state that the number of wearable devices worldwide more than doubled between 2016 & 2019 from 325 million to 722 million, with a forecast of more than 1 billion by 2022.

Source Statista 2021.

Type of tech	2018 (millions)	2022 (millions)
Watch	72.4	121.1
Band	44.2	45.5
Clothing	2.9	10.5
Earwear	2.1	12.3
Modular	0.8	0.7

+ other (glasses) 0.2m. both years.

Total wearable shipments

- 2018 – 122.6 million
- 2022 – 190.4 million

* All figures represent millions

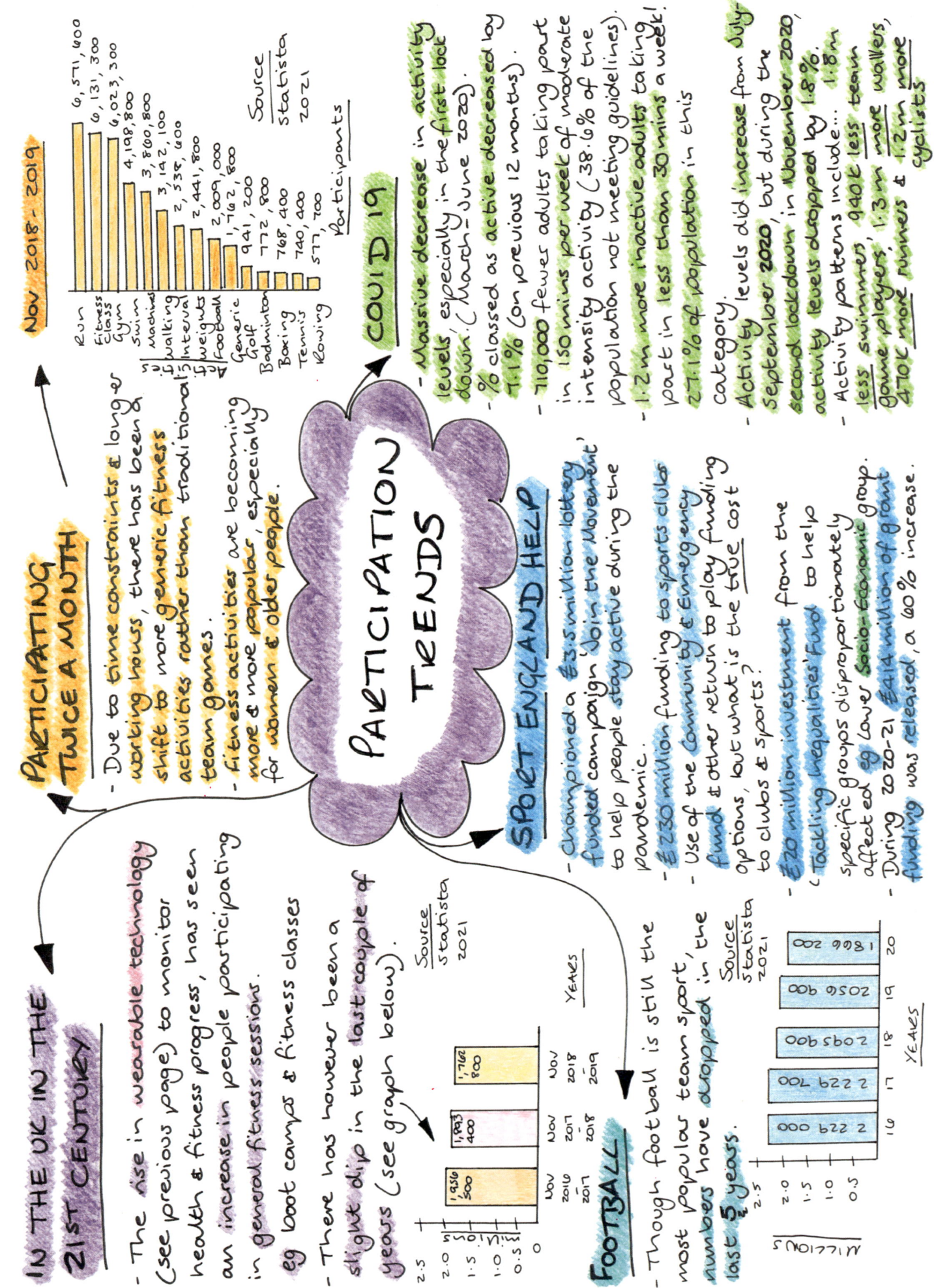

PARTICIPATION TRENDS

IN THE UK IN THE 21ST CENTURY
- The rise in wearable technology (see previous page) to monitor health & fitness progress, has seen an increase in people participating in general fitness sessions.
eg boot camps & fitness classes
- There has however been a slight dip in the last couple of years (see graph below).

Source Statista 2021

Bar graph (millions / Years):
Nov 2016–2017: 1,956,500
Nov 2017–2018: 1,883,400
Nov 2018–2019: 1,762,800

PARTICIPATING TWICE A MONTH
- Due to time constraints & longer working hours, there has been a shift to more generic fitness activities rather than traditional team games.
- Fitness activities are becoming more & more popular, especially for women & older people.

Bar graph (Nov 2018–2019, Participants):
- Run — 6,571,400
- Fitness Class — 6,131,300
- Gym — 6,023,300
- Swim — 4,198,800
- Machines — 3,800,800
- Walking — 3,142,100
- Interval — 2,538,400
- Weights — 2,441,800
- Football — 2,009,000
- Generic — 1,762,800
- Golf — 941,200
- Badminton — 772,800
- Boxing — 768,400
- Tennis — 740,400
- Rowing — 577,700

Source Statista 2021

COVID 19
- Massive decrease in activity levels, especially in the first lockdown (March–June 2020).
- % classed as active decreased by 7.1% (on previous 12 months).
- 710,000 fewer adults taking part in 150 mins per week of moderate intensity activity (38.6% of the population not meeting guidelines).
- 1.2m more inactive adults taking part in less than 30 mins a week. 27.1% of population in this category.
- Activity levels did increase from July–September 2020, but during the second lockdown in November 2020, activity levels dropped by 1.8%.
- Activity patterns include... 1.8m less swimmers, 940k less team game players, 1.3m more walkers & 1.2m more cyclists

SPORT ENGLAND HELP
- Championed a £35.5 million lottery funded campaign 'join the movement' to help people stay active during the pandemic.
- £230 million funding to sports clubs
- Use of the community & emergency fund & others return to play funding options, but what is the true cost to clubs & sports?
- £20 million investment from the 'Tackling Inequalities Fund' to help specific groups disproportionately affected eg lower socio-economic group.
- During 2020-21 £414 million of grant funding was released, a 60% increase.

FOOTBALL
- Though football is still the most popular team sport, numbers have dropped in the last 5 years.

Source Statista 2021

Bar graph (millions / Years):
Nov 16: 2,229,000
Nov 17: 2,229,700
Nov 18: 2,095,900
Nov 19: 2,056,900
Nov 20: 1,866,200

Topic 5: Sport and Society

1. **Discuss** the differences in sporting pursuits of the different social classes pre-industrial Britain. **(8 marks)**

2. **Analyse** the impact of the industrial revolution on the development of organised sport. **(8 marks)**

3. **Discuss** how public schools and universities in the 19th century influenced the development of games in society? **(8 marks)**

4. **Explain** how corporation teams have changed how professional sporting competitions operate? **(6 marks)**

5. **State** 3 disadvantages of the migration of sporting labour. **(3 marks)**

6. **Suggest** reasons why opportunities to participate in sport and recreational activities has improved for specific target groups in the last two decades? **(6 marks)**

7. **Explain** the impact the British Empire had on the development of sport in various colonised countries. **(6 marks)**

8. **Assess** the impact of hosting global games has on the host country. **(8 marks)**

9. **Explain** the historical developments as a result of the industrial revolution that led to an increase in commercialisation of sport. **(6 marks)**

10. **Describe** what is meant by the 'golden triangle'? **(3 marks)**

11. Peter Ueberroth is credited with creating the blueprint for commercialisation in sport. **Explain** this statement. (6 marks)

12. **Discuss** the impact of franchises in elite sport. (8 marks)

13. **Describe** the difference between sportsmanship to gamesmanship? (2 marks)

14. **State** reasons why performers engage in deviant behaviour at elite level? (4 marks)

15. Using examples, **describe** two ways in which performers can act in a deviant manner in sport. (4 marks)

16. **Explain** two ways in which WADA attempts to combat against the use of PEDs. (4 marks)

17. **Summarise** how technology has had an impact on:
    a. Development of player standards (2 marks)
    b. The viewing experience for spectators. (4 marks)

18. **Assess** the impact the former East German talent ID model on the current UK ID model. (8 marks)

19. **Define** mass participation. (1 mark)

20. **Discuss** the impact wearable technology has had on mass participation in physical activity and sport. (8 marks)

Total Marks: /113